Tortoise

Animal

Series editor: Jonathan Burt

Already published

Crow
Boria Sax

Ant
Charlotte Sleigh

Cockroach
Marion Copeland

Forthcoming

Tortoise

Peter Young

REAKTION BOOKS

For Timothy Tortoise: 50 years in the family

Published by
REAKTION BOOKS LTD
79 Farringdon Road
London EC1M 3JU, UK
www.reaktionbooks.co.uk

First published 2003
Copyright © Peter Young, 2003

Printed in China

British Library Cataloguing in Publication Data

Young, Peter
    Tortoise. – (Animal)
    1. Tortoise 2. Animals and civilization
    I. Title
    597.9'2

    ISBN 1 86189 191 1

Contents

Albert van der Eeckhout, *Two Brazilian Tortoises* (c. 1640).

1 Fittest not Fastest

Tortoises look and are old, almost mythical creatures. They are primeval, the oldest of the living land reptiles, their age confirmed by fossil remains. Tortoises are the surviving link between animal life in water and on land. Some 280 million years ago, late in the Carboniferous period when coal was being formed from rotting vegetation in forest swamps, reptiles were the first creatures to emerge and breed on land.

So named from the Latin *reptilis* (creeping), reptiles as a class developed to survive in a dry environment. Fins became strong legs; they had tough skins, jaws that enabled them to eat plants, and they laid durable eggs. Their presence on land led to a cycle of improvement. For example, as herbivores they ate seeds that passed undamaged through the gut and were deposited complete with fertiliser, thus increasing the animals' food supply. Gradually they came to be the lords of creation, ending the dominance of marine creatures within the animal kingdom. The Age of the Reptiles was a long one, from about 245 to 65 million years ago. During that time, though, many species died out, to reappear only as museum skeletons or reconstructions in virtual reality. Tortoises, which emerged early in that period, have survived for some 225 million years. They are living fossils. Hardy, self-contained creatures, they have endured aeons of major changes,

Resembling fossils, tortoises have also inspired jokes about mating with rocks.

and on a world scale survived geological upheaval, volcanic activity and climatic swings.

It is not difficult to see why they have survived. The obvious reason is that they have an external skeleton, a bony shell that boxes them in. This evolved over time. Originally, to protect their flesh, the creatures grew a series of horny plates or scales. In response to threats these became larger, eventually joining together to create the shell as we know it today. During this process, the skin and muscles of the back and breast had a diminishing function, gradually wasting away to the point where the shell was resting on the bones. Ultimately, most of the internal bones fused with the living bone casing, leaving the bones of the neck and tail free.

Most tortoises have a high domed shell, a carapace that is strong and hard to crack. A literal translation of the German *Schildkröte* is shield-toad, and of the Hungarian *teknösbéka* bowl-frog. In Corsican, a language akin to Italian, the word for tortoise, *cupulatta*, both echoes its shape and suggests its stomping gait. The dome shape is difficult for predators to get their jaws around. It does have a disadvantage, though, should the creatures when climbing tumble back on to it. All they can do is wave their legs helplessly in the air, trying to right themselves. Rescue can come only from some outsider tipping them over. An exception is the pancake tortoise. With its flat shell and unusual agility, it can flip itself over quickly when it lands on its back, a common occurrence when climbing in its natural East African habitats.

Made up of interlocking horny plates called scutes (Latin: *scutum*, shield), the shell stays the same shape as the tortoises increase in size. Of all the protective measures adopted within the animal kingdom, it is one of the surest. It is not an absolute protection, but it deters many predators. Indeed, a tortoise's

Our defence is sure. Tortoises have survived for millions of years by operating undercover.

shell is not unlike a soldier's helmet. The Roman historian Livy has Titus Quinctius addressing the Achaeans in 191 BC:

> . . . like a tortoise, which I see to be secure against all attacks, when it has all its parts drawn up inside its shell, but when it sticks any part out of it has that member which is exposed weak and open to injury.[1]

Like soldiers, too, tortoises are often camouflaged, the pattern of their shells blending in with their environment for extra safety. For example, the little Egyptian tortoise has a yellowish tan shell, whereas so-called Greek tortoises look more like brown earth. The under-shell, the plastron, is lighter in colour.

The young soft-shelled are still at risk, as were the giant tortoises on remote Indian and Pacific Ocean islands. Having no natural enemies before man, they could afford, in evolutionary terms to reduce considerably the bony part of their shells, which were not particularly hard. Nevertheless, they could be

TANZANIA 50/-
PANCAKE TORTOISE
(Malacochersus tornieri)

TANZANIA 20/-
PANCAKE TORTOISE
(Malacochersus tornieri)

TANZANIA 70/-
PANCAKE
TORTOISE HATCHLING
(Malacochersus tornieri)

TANZANIA 30/-
PANCAKE TORTOISE
(Malacochersus tornieri)

Hiding from predators, the pancake tortoise is one of the less visible creatures of East Africa.

used as stepping-stones. It was claimed that on Galapagos they were so numerous that it was possible to walk quite long distances on their backs without touching the ground.

When first discovered, the African pancake tortoise was thought to be underdeveloped and malformed. Its shell is flat, less than 4 centimetres high, and soft, yielding under pressure. An agile climber, it lives on rocky slopes in Kenya, Tanzania (including Serengeti National Park) and the *kopjes* of southeastern Africa, where it runs for cover rather than retreating into its shell when threatened. Its lighter shell enables it to run faster than tortoises with a thick shell. Hiding under a rocky crevice, it breathes in deeply like a bullfrog, increasing its size so that it is wedged and almost impossible to pull out by hand.[2]

Bell's hinge-back tortoise lives in the dry savannahs of Central Africa.

The hinge-back tortoise of Central and Southern Africa normally rests with its head drawn into the front of its shell. To protect its back, it has a unique hinge like the visor on a helmet. Located in line with the second and third back-plates, this allows the rear of the carapace to be lowered in the event of its being attacked. Box tortoises, native to North America, are able to close up completely.

In the witty view of the Revd Sydney Smith (1771–1845), the carapace made the creatures insensitive. When a child stooped down to stroke the shell of a turtle he asked why. The child answered: 'To please the turtle.' To which Sydney replied: 'Why, you might as well stroke the dome of St Paul's to please the Dean and Chapter.'[3]

In times of danger, the creatures can quickly retract their vulnerable parts, the head and legs, into the shell. The bowsprit tortoise is well adapted for this, with a particularly small front opening of the carapace. Where the front legs are exposed they are protected by thick scales. Having no ear openings, tortoises

11

The American boxed tortoise shuts down at the front.

The leopard tortoise, found in the savannahs from the Sudan and the Horn of Africa to the Cape and the north in South-western Africa to Angola, won't change his spots.

do not hear well. When the eighteenth-century naturalist Gilbert White (1720–1793) called loudly to his pet, Timothy, through a speaking trumpet, Timothy 'did not seem to regard the noise'. Danger is signalled by sudden movement and alarm is expressed by a sharp hiss. Charles Darwin (1809–1882) observed the giant species on the Galapagos Islands in September 1835:

> The inhabitants believe that these animals are absolutely deaf; certainly they do not overhear a person walking close behind them. I was always amused, when overtaking one of these great monsters as it was quietly pacing along, to see how suddenly, the instant I passed, it would draw in its head and legs, and uttering a deep hiss fall to the ground with a heavy sound, as if struck dead. I frequently got on their backs, and then, upon giving a few raps on the hinder part of the shell, they would rise up and walk away; but I found it very difficult to keep my balance.[4]

One of the advantages that giant tortoises have is being able to stretch their necks and legs to expose parasites, which birds pick off. Galapagos tortoises, for instance, tend to have ticks, which finches eat.

Tortoises live in warm climates, and they are native to all continents except Australasia. Being cold-blooded, or more correctly poikilotherms, they depend on their surroundings to maintain body temperature, seeking warmth when cold and avoiding it if in danger of overheating. For instance, North American gopher tortoises, distinguished by their dull flat shells, live in the dry sandy wastes of the southern United States, where daytime temperatures are unbearable. Gophers (from the French *gaufre*, honeycomb) spend much of the day and night in

Oswald is getting Drowsy

Happy helps him along

J. F. Horrabin, creator of the Japhet and Happy characters, took sleep as his theme for this strip.

the burrows they excavate with their heavily scaled flattened forefeet, efficient for digging. Tunnels more than 12 metres long have been recorded. At the end is a chamber where humidity and temperature are relatively constant. It is also a refuge during forest fires. Snakes, frogs, owls and rodents may also shelter in what can become a maze of tunnels. Gophers, whose lifestyle was captured in Walt Disney's Oscar-winning documentary *The Living Desert* (1953), typically emerge at dawn to feed on succulents in the cool of the morning.

In their natural habitats tortoises get plenty of rest. After emptying their digestive tracts to prevent a build-up of toxins, they hibernate for months below the frost zone, because frost can blind them. Gently ticking over in slumber, they are unaware of the miseries of winter weather, ice and snow and storms. In the Northern hemisphere they naturally have a quiet Christmas. (A wild British group hibernates in the bunkers of a Welsh golf-course.) What the sensation of coming to after hibernation is like to the creature we cannot know, but Edgar Allan Poe (1809–1849) offers a possible comparison in 'The Premature Burial' (1844):

There arrived an epoch – as often there had arrived – in which I found myself emerging from total uncon-sciousness into the first feeble and indefinite sense of existence. Slowly – with a tortoise gradation – approached the faint gray dawn of the psychal day. A torpid uneasiness. An apathetic endurance of dull pain. No care – no hope – no effort. Then, after a long interval, a ringing in the ears; then, after a lapse still longer, a pricking or tingling sensation in the extremities; then a seemingly eternal period of pleasurable quiescence, during which the awakening feelings are struggling into thought; then a brief re-sinking into non-entity; then a sudden recovery. At length the slight quivering of an eyelid, and immediately thereupon, an electric shock of a terror, deadly and indefinite, which sends the blood in torrents from the temples to the heart. And now the first positive effort to think. And now the first endeavour to remember. And now a partial and evanescent success. And now the memory has so far regained its dominion, that, in some measure, I am cognizant of my state. I feel that I am not awaking from ordinary sleep. I recollect that I have been subject to catalepsy.

In 1947, on the only visit by a reigning monarch to St Helena, King George VI bowed to Jonathan. The sole survivor of that royal party is Queen Elizabeth (second from right), who succeeded her father in 1953. Jonathan has gone on to appear on a local 5 pence coin (1998) and a 5 pence stamp in 2003.

To many tortoise lovers, awaking from hibernation is an annual miracle. For six to ten weeks in the wild and up to six months as pets in cooler climes, the creatures have lived without taking fluid or food and their static limbs have not seized up or wasted away. Their annual cycle is carefully regulated. For a few weeks before going into hibernation they cease eating and clear their systems of waste matter so that it does not decay within them. They are then ready to use their forelegs as side-scrapers to dig themselves in for the winter.

During the summer they sleep at night and in the heat of the day. Basking in warm, but not too hot, spots is a favourite pastime. Their seasonal and daily routines, regulated by a highly developed body clock and ambient temperatures, make for an energy-saving life. The Revd L. P. Walcott summed it up neatly in 1924 after meeting at the St Helena governor's house Jonathan, a tortoise reputed to have been on the island when Napoleon was exiled there (1815–21):

Said I to the Tortoise, 'How old may you be?'
'Two hundred or so,' said the Tortoise to me.
'That's a very long time,' to the Tortoise I said.
'Not so long,' he replied, 'for most was in bed.'

The clergyman went on to observe: 'There was a world of accumulated experience and shrewd wisdom in those bright peering eyes and wrinkled head as he watched the human butterflies flitting about on the lawn.'[5] In fact, Jonathan, a giant tortoise from the Seychelles, did not arrive on St Helena until 1882, 61 years after Napoleon's death. He is the sole survivor of three giant tortoises that arrived in St Helena in the nineteenth century. On arrival, Jonathan was thought to be mature, that is, about 50 years old.

Sir James Harford, a governor of the island, wrote a charming piece about Jonathan in 1959:

Surely no other living creature could more impressively figure as the symbol of venerable antiquity, or perhaps advance a better claim to the majestic position of doyen of the animal kingdom on earth . . . His regime is marked by an immense slowness and sameness. He moves little in the course of a day, at his speed of half a mile to the hour, each step with all four legs being an achievement requiring several seconds for its accomplishment. It is impossible to live for years with Jonathan without developing an affection for him – but it is not reciprocated; he appears to be totally impersonal, and almost free from emotions of any kind. His nervous stability is enviable, his gravitas truly Roman, and his phlegm more than British . . . Most firmly impressed upon the memory is the image of Jonathan, the portentous herbivore, patient, ponderous, prehistoric, as upon that wide green expanse, harmonising so fittingly with his placid island environment, all day long as he browses and drowses, lumbers and slumbers.[6]

He also bathes in and drinks from the water trough in the corner of the paddock. At the governor's annual garden party in the grounds of Plantation House, Jonathan, apparently sightless in one eye, lumbers towards Guides, perhaps attracted by their uniforms. He loves attention. In 1998 he featured on a local coin.

Tortoise constitutions are made for conservation. During months of hibernation not a drop of fluid is taken in. In his *Natural History* (77 AD), the Roman writer Pliny the Elder noted:

There are also turtles living on land, and consequently called in works on the subject terrestrial species; these are found in the deserts of Africa in the region of the driest and most arid sands, and it is believed they live on the moisture of dew. No other animal occurs there.[7]

Charles Darwin was able to make a more direct observation during his five weeks on Galapagos, which takes its name from the Spanish word for freshwater terrapin:

The tortoise is very fond of water, drinking large quantities, and wallowing in the mud. The larger islands alone possess springs, and these are always situated towards the central parts, and at a considerable elevation. The tortoises, therefore, which frequent the lower districts, when thirsty, are obliged to travel from a long distance. Hence broad and well-beaten paths radiate off in every direction from the wells even down to the sea-coast; and the Spaniards by following them up, first discovered the watering-places. When I landed at Chatham Island, I could not imagine what animal travelled so methodically along the well-chosen tracks. Near the springs it was a curious spectacle to behold many of these great monsters; one set eagerly travelling onwards with outstretched necks, and another set returning, after having drunk their fill. When the tortoise arrives at the spring, quite regardless of any spectator, it buries its head in the water above its eyes, and greedily swallows great mouthfuls, at the rate of about ten in a minute . . . I believe it is well ascertained, that the bladder of the frog acts as a reservoir for the moisture necessary for its existence: such seems to be the case with the tortoise. For some time after a visit to the springs, the urinary bladder of these animals is distended with fluid, which is said gradually to decrease in volume, and to become less pure. The inhabitants, when walking in the lower district, and overcome with thirst, often take advantage of this circumstance, by killing a tortoise, and if the bladder is full, drinking its contents. In one I saw killed, the fluid was quite limpid, and had only a very slightly bitter taste. The inhabitants, however, always drink first the water in the pericardium, which is described as being best.[8]

A female tortoise can slow or stop her reproduction process at will. She can retain male sperm inside her body for as long as two years before letting it fertilize her eggs. Growth of the egg can be halted for a similar period. If there is inadequate food, the female can reabsorb her own egg or withhold laying until conditions have improved. Laid eggs are white and round, in smaller species resembling ping-pong balls. One

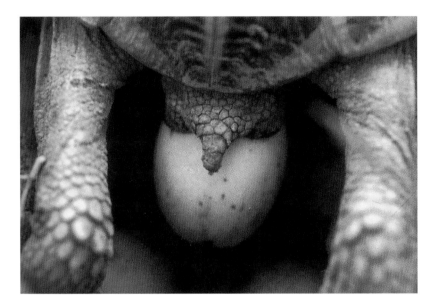

Eggs resemble ping-pong balls.

measured by Darwin was 'seven inches and three-eighths in circumference'.

Regarded as slow creatures, like their heart rate, tortoises are a byword for sluggish movement, as in tortoise-footed or tortoise pace. In Shakespeare's play *The Tempest*, Prospero's first command to his savage and deformed slave Caliban is 'Come, thou tortoise!' (i. ii. 316). Alexander Theroux (*b*. 1939) makes the contrast in 'The tortoise of the hour hand, the hare of the minute hand' (*OED*, under 'tortoise'). A tortoise race is one in which the last person home wins. In his *Letters from the Earth*, Mark Twain commented on sexual lethargy:

> But the Bible doesn't allow adultery at all, whether a person can help it or not. It allows no distinction between goat and tortoise – the excitable goat, the emotional goat,

that has some adultery every day or fade and die; and the
tortoise, that calm cold puritan, that takes a treat only
once in two years and then goes to sleep in the midst of it
and doesn't wake up for sixty days.[9]

The concave
plastron of the
male enables
him to mount
females.

Females have been reported as continuing to eat for quite a
while before noticing that a male has mounted.

The colder it is, the slower the reaction. Nevertheless, in
reasonable temperatures the creatures can move fairly quickly,
especially if threatened. Darwin in his journal again:

The tortoises, when moving towards any definite point,
travel by night, and arrive at their journey's end much
sooner than would be expected. The inhabitants, from
observations on marked individuals, consider that they

'Maniac!!' – a turn of speed by American cartoonist John Bell.

can move a distance of about eight miles in two or three days. One large tortoise, which I watched, I found walked at the rate of sixty yards in ten minutes, that is 360 in the hour, or four miles a day, allowing also a little time for it to eat on the road.[10]

Smaller species are much slower and cover smaller distances. For instance, a woman who forgot her tortoise when she moved a mile away was surprised to see it turn up at her new house seven years later. Over time longer distances can be covered. One wanderer was returned from the middle of Hendon aerodrome near London, having crossed some fields and the Watford bypass, scaled an embankment, clambered over or under various railway lines, and eluded Royal Air Force sentries in his descent.

Tortoises are basically mute, except for males squealing with delight, sometimes with open mouth, at the climax of mating.

In compensation for not hearing well they have well-developed senses of seeing, smelling and tasting, which all help in the selection of food. They sniff well and can be attracted from some distance by the smell, for instance, of ripe fruit.

The ideal tortoise diet is low in protein and fat, yet high in complex carbohydrate, fibre and natural calcium and adequate in other minerals such as phosphate and vitamins. Calcium is important for building shell and skeleton, especially in the young, egg production in laying females and muscular function. Buttercups, clover, dandelion, honeysuckle, plantains, sow thistles and similar plants provide dietary fibre in the wild. Being poikilotherms, tortoises are able to digest their food only if they are eating in the right ambient temperature, ideally within the range of 20–32°C. Outside this range, they become sluggish, can experience physiological stress, eat less than they need, digest it inefficiently and increase the risk of succumbing to disease. On islands with sparse food, they have evolved with long legs and a shell raised above the neck so that they can reach and browse on higher vegetation, as Darwin saw on Galapagos:

> The tortoises which live on those islands where there is no water, or in the lower and arid parts of the others, chiefly feed on succulent cactus. Those which frequent the higher and damp regions, eat the leaves of various trees, a kind of berry (called guayavita) which is acid and austere, and likewise a pale green filamentous lichen, that hangs in tresses from the boughs of the trees.[11]

Tortoises have been known to knock over small trees and shrubs in their search for tasty leaves.

Collecting specimens in the Cameroons, the naturalist Gerald Durrell (1925–1995) found that they refused the ripe

This hatchling will quickly have to fend for itself. Surviving in the Amazon forest, it could reach a length of 80 cm.

fruit and tender leaves he offered them. A native hunter advised him that the creatures lived on a species of tiny white forest mushrooms that grew on dead tree trunks. Fed these mushrooms, the tortoises gained an appetite for other food, gave up eating mushrooms altogether and much preferred a nice ripe mango.[12] Another appreciated fruit is bananas, eaten skin and all. One item in the wild the healthy-eating herbivores are partial to is dung, from camels, goats and sheep.

Kept as European pets, they eat food that would not be found in the wild. One in Britain with the Pickwickian name of Mr Snodgrass – because he ate grass – was also fond of green peas, defrosted of course, strawberries and raspberries. He ate bread and milk but preferred the sweetness of cherry cake dipped in milk. Another tucked into crushed snails, which, like the shoe-whitening preparation on tennis shoes, contained calcium. Likewise crushed bone such as oyster shell or grated cuttlefish. Tennis shoes themselves attract jaws, as do nail-varnished toes mistaken for favourite fruits. A vermilion varnish can be taken for a piece of tomato. As anybody who has allowed a finger too close to a tortoise's mouth will testify, they have a strong, tenacious bite that can draw blood, leaving a clear indent in the shape of the creature's jaw.

For one called Oswald a special delicacy was the leaves of the ice plant, but during the runner-bean season he would follow his owner around the garden almost asking for beans, though he preferred them sliced. Another was particularly fond of snapdragons. Young cabbage plants, fallen currants, foxgloves and marigold leaves have also been reported as tasty for tortoises. In the 1930s one dealer claimed to potential customers that his tortoises were trained to leave lettuces alone.

Like humans, tortoises can be particular about their diets, but plenty of advice on what is good for them is to be had from associations of tortoise keepers, booklets on reptile care, vets and similar sources. Cucumber and lettuce are favoured for their high moisture content. Some lettuces, for example lollo rosso, are high in flavonols, which are very effective anti-oxidants. These fight free radicals, which damage cells and hasten ageing. Many experts argue that lettuce as a staple diet is unnatural and, being largely cellulose, lacks nutrition. In general, the darker greens such as watercress, broccoli, cress and grated dark-green cabbages are to be preferred. Above all, variety is the key to a good diet. Researchers at Zurich Zoo, where 29 Galapagos tortoises are kept, in 2000 found that four-year-old offspring were growing too quickly, weighing ten times more than those in the wild. They were prescribed a high fibre diet.[13]

The herbivorous high-fibre diet is healthy, enabling tortoises to live up to 150 years. There are records of individuals living longer. A claim is made for Tui Malilia, the tortoise reputed to have been presented to the Queen of Tonga by Captain Cook in 1773 or 1777, and long honoured as a chief. Dying in 1966, he merited a fourth leader in *The Times*, a paper that often sang the praises of the species.[14] Having survived a forest fire and the kick of a horse, he would have been at least 189 years old, but he may have been one in a succession of the species and Captain Cook never visited his homeland, Madagascar. The creatures cannot be accurately dated by the number of rings, which are evidence not of annual but of variable dietary or seasonal growth. Within a year there may be four or five growing seasons.

The oldest reliable record is of a Marion's tortoise imported by the Chevalier de Fresne into Mauritius from Aldabra in 1766, when the native species were becoming extinct through being taken for food. Marion's tortoises were important enough to be mentioned in the Treaty of 1810, when Mauritius was ceded to Britain by the French. Legend has it that the large dent on the right side of the survivor's shell came from a shot fired by British guns just before the island was ceded. The British Government seems not to have contributed directly to its upkeep, and it was looked after at the Royal Artillery barracks in the capital, Port Louis.[15] Josephine de la Bere recalled in 1930:

I remember as a young girl in 1877 guests at the Royal Artillery Mess were given a ride on the large tortoise, and the Commander Royal Artillery of the time always rode to dinner on it – quite a little ceremony. It was said then to be over 100 years old.[16]

A small boy rode across the barrack square on it and, so strong was the creature, that a photograph was taken of the tortoise walking about quite comfortably with a notoriously stout officer of the regiment and two others on its back. Later in life it 'was not a willing aid to the locomotion of passengers'. Once, when it was off colour, soapy water from the washbasins got into its concrete pond, which sappers had constructed after the medical officer had condemned the muddy area in which it liked to wallow as a mosquito-breeding place. Whatever was in the soap acted as an immediate pick-me-up. Eventually it went blind and died in a fall down a well in 1918 at the age of at least 152. In their natural state tortoises tend to lose their sight and die of accidents, such as falling over a precipice. The stuffed giant tortoise of Mauritius is preserved in the Natural History Museum in London, with a cast as a memorial in Port Louis.

Timothy, hatched around 1842, is the leading contender for the British record as the Methuselah of the animal kingdom. As a hatchling she would have had to fend for herself. She was rescued from a Portuguese brigantine in the Mediterranean, perhaps part of the cargo, by a British naval captain and was on HMS *Queen* at the bombardment of Sebastopol during the Crimean War in 1855, later seeing action in the East Indies and China. Since 1914 she has lived in retirement at Powderham Castle, the seat of the Earls of Devon. Her favourite foods are wisteria flowers, dandelion leaves and strawberries, a recommendation for vegetarianism. To date, she has outlived seven earls. To protect her from inquisitive members of the public visiting the castle, she has a card attached to her shell: 'My name is Timothy. I am very old. Please do not pick me up.'[17] Another Mediterranean tortoise in Britain is Joey, guessed to have hatched around 1800. Although one cannot be certain about his early history, he is probably older than 160.

Because tortoises are likely to outlive their owners, they are mentioned in wills, receiving modest bequests. Small legacies also ensure a continuing supply of a creature's favourite food. For instance, in 1957 Mrs Emily Wilson of Doncaster, Yorkshire, left in her will of £30,000 a bequest of £100 to her maidservant Mary L. Guy and 'my tortoise, in the firm belief that she will look after and maintain the same'. Christina Foyle, the London bookshop owner, was more generous to her tortoises than to her family. In her will of £59 million she left £20,000 for the care of her pets, including six tortoises. Along with the tortoises, her former gardener, Tony Scillitoe, received £100,000, double the amount left to any family member. A stipulation was that the care of the animals should continue for 21 years after her death, in 1999.[18]

The record weight, 385 kilograms, is of a Galapagos tortoise at the Life Fellowship Bird Sanctuary in Florida. Appropriately called Goliath, it also holds the record for the longest shell, 1.36 metres.[19] The smallest is the speckled sape or speckled padloper, which has not exceeded 9.6 centimetres.

The most famous pet is another Timothy, owned by Gilbert White, curate and naturalist, who included him in his *Natural History and Antiquities of Selborne* (1789). Timothy, collected in Algiers about 1739–40, was bought from a sailor in Chichester, Sussex, for half a crown by Mrs Rebecca Snooke, White's paternal aunt, who lived in the east side of Sussex, at Ringmer. She looked after Timothy, feeding him kidney beans and cucumbers within her walled garden, where he dug himself into a border for the winters. On her death in 1780, White inherited Timothy, gave him the run of his five-acre garden and studied his personality, noting his diet, habits and weight. For example, on 17 October 1782 White entered in his journal:

The tortoise not only gets into the sun under the fruit-wall; but he tilts one edge of his shell against the wall, so as to incline his back to it's [sic] rays: by which contrivance he obtains more heat than if he lay in his natural position. And yet this poor reptile has never read, that planes inclining to the horizon receive more heat from the sun than any other elevation. At four p.m. he retires to bed under the broad foliage of a hollyhock. He has ceased to eat for some time.[20]

Gilbert White's notes on 'the old Sussex tortoise' go right up to the month of his death in 1793, the final journal entry on 1 June being: 'Timothy is very voracious: when he can get no other food he eats grass in the walks'.[21] By the following spring Timothy, who had been losing weight for four years, followed his master to his grave like a faithful dog. His carapace was presented to the British Museum of Natural History in 1853. He may also be seen in Selborne parish church in the centre roundel of the three-light bicentennial memorial window to Gilbert White, 'a faithful priest, a humble student of nature and a writer of genius'. Unlikely as it would have seemed, White's *Natural History* was to become the fourth most published book in the English language.

Hitherto, the study of tortoises had been largely confined to observations of singular characteristics. White's record was the most continuous to date, a bachelor's domestic document lovingly revealing everything about Timothy except his age and sex. His age was unknown and he was in fact female. Fittingly, in the 1836 edition of the *Natural History*, the editor identified Timothy as an independent species, giving her the name *Testudo whitei*, or Gilbert White's tortoise.

In the nineteenth and early twentieth centuries, there was a more systematic and international recording and classification. One of the facets of the British Empire was the exploration of

Edward Lear, known for his Nonsense verse, was also an accomplished illustrator, as this example of an angulate tortoise shows. It appeared in J. E. Gray's *Tortoises, Terrapins and Turtles Drawn from Life* (1872)

TESTUDO ANGULATA.

territories, followed by the acquisition of exotic species, arte-facts and knowledge, which were then dutifully displayed, recorded and published. For example, in 1824 John Edward Gray (1800–1875) was engaged by John George Children to assist in preparing a catalogue of the British Museum reptile collection. This appeared in 1844. Gray also published *Synopsis Reptilium; or, Short Descriptions of the Species of Reptiles* (1831). He succeeded Children in 1840 as keeper of the zoological department, and in 1853 invited Albert Günther (1830–1914) to prepare a catalogue of the amphibia and reptiles in the Museum. Günther also published *Geographical Distribution of Reptiles* (1858), *The Reptiles of British India* (1864) and *The Gigantic Land-Tortoises (Living and Extinct) in the Collection of the British Museum* (1877). Succeeding Gray as keeper of the zoological department, he established the zoological library.

Thomas Bell (1792–1880), dental surgeon and zoologist, made a major contribution to tortoise studies, publishing *A Monograph of Testudinata* (1832–6), *History of British Reptiles* (1839) and 'On Chelonia of London Clay' in his *Fossil Reptilia of London Clay* (1849). From 1830 the boom in building the railway network, with London as its hub, including the digging of cuttings and the construction of tunnels, had unearthed much fossil evidence, as had earlier excavations for the canal network. Plates for the *Monograph* appeared as *Tortoises and Turtles* (1872), the drawings by the nature artist James Sowerby being lithographed by Edward Lear, famed for his nonsense verse. Bell retired to Selborne, buying Gilbert White's house from his great-nieces, collecting relics and memorabilia of White and producing in 1876–7 his classic two-volume edition of *Natural History of Selborne*.

In 1865 Mordecai Cubitt (1825–1914) produced *Our Reptiles: A Plain . . . Account of the Lizards, Snakes, Newts, Toads,*

Frogs and Tortoises Indigenous to Great Britain and in 1875 Charles Harrt published *Amazonian Tortoise Myths*. Lord Rothschild (1868–1937) kept a 'Book Register of Tortoise Measurements' (1896, a manuscript kept at Tring, Hertfordshire). After engaging in correspondence and gathering notes, he wrote *The Gigantic Land Tortoises of the Galapagos Archipelago* (1907) and *The Gigantic Land Tortoises of the Seychelles, etc.* (1915).

The American authority was Raymond Lee Ditmars (1876–1942), curator of mammals and reptiles at New York Zoological Park. His main publications were *The Reptile Book: A Review of the Crocodilians, Lizards, Snakes, Turtles and Tortoises Inhabiting the United States and Northern Mexico, etc.* (1907), *Reptiles of the World: Tortoises and Turtles, Crocodilians, Lizards and Snakes of the Eastern and Western Hemispheres* (1910) and *The Reptiles of North America* (1936), an update of his work of 1907.

Advances in zoology were helped by developments in the new branch of geology, palaeontology. In 1816 the canal engineer William Smith first pointed out in his *Strata Identified by Organised Fossils* the succession of fauna and their utility in determining the relative ages of deposits. A country doctor, Gideon Mantell (1790–1852) established in *Fossils of the South Downs* (1822) that, along with the remains of giant lizards, the fossils of Stonesfield in Oxfordshire and near Cuckfield in the Sussex Weald included 'bones and plates of several species of Tortoise'.[22] In 1831 Mantell elaborated his ideas on the position of fossils within the sequence of rocks in a paper, 'The Geographical Age of the Reptiles'. It was the first to set out in detail the evidence for the order in which these creatures had appeared in what would later be called the Mesozoic era.[23] From 1830 Charles Lyell had argued in his *Principles of Geology* that the earth was millions rather than a few thousand years old.

Appropriately, tortoises are table numbers in the Origins Bar and Bistro, Darwin College, The University of Kent at Canterbury.

In 1834 the term palaeontology was first used. The following year the Scottish palaeontologist Hugh Falconer discovered in the Punjab the remains of a giant tortoise, colossochelys, with a shell more than 2 metres long. Meanwhile (1831–6), after an entomologist curate had turned down the opportunity, Darwin in his early twenties was sailing as a naturalist aboard HMS *Beagle*. During the voyage he was profoundly influenced by Lyell's book, with its notion of gradual geological change: 'The great merit of Principles was that it altered the whole tone of one's mind.' At first, contrary to the assertions of the Galapagos natives that a tortoise could be assigned to its island by its shell shape, he thought that they were buccaneers' food imports. Acknowledging the shift in thought, a portrait of Lyell was to be the principal one of three mentors above the fireplace in Darwin's study at Down House, Kent, where after physical exercise for thought he sat in an armchair and put his theory on paper. More than twenty years after his basic field research, his application of Lyell's approach and his own findings on the voyage were to have a profound effect on human thought.

By the middle of the nineteenth century, the relative, but not yet the absolute, geologic timescale was substantially complete. With it grew palaeontological evidence. For example, in 1878 miners working in a shaft of the Saint Barbara colliery at Bernissart near Mons, Belgium, found at a depth of 322 metres fragments of what at first were believed to be fossilized wood. They proved to be the mass grave of nearly 30 iguanodons, dinosaurs of the type discovered in the 1820s by Gideon Mantell and his wife in the Sussex Weald, and along with them were also two types of tortoise, the larger having a total length of 25 centimetres. The find was dated to the Middle Cretaceous period, about 135 million years ago.

The first turtles and tortoises appeared some 225 million years ago, in the Triassic Period, which lasted for about 35 million years, during which the climate changed globally from warm and wet to hotter and drier. At the end of the Triassic, the first dinosaurs, small creatures measured in centimetres, and the first true mammals appeared. Dinosaurs, species of which would grow to a length of 27 metres and a weight of 75 tonnes, were destined to die out about 65 million years ago. Mammals were set to evolve. Turtles and tortoises as an order would evolve and survive.

There is much speculation as to why dinosaurs became extinct reptiles after dominating the earth for perhaps 150 million years. Theories include geological and climatic change, perhaps intensified by volcanic activity, affecting habitat and food supply; small brain power in relation to size; and failure in the process of natural selection to adapt against the rising class of mammals. Recent theories suggest a burst of deadly gamma radiation or the impact of an asteroid or swarm of comets, which would increase carbon dioxide levels and create an environment alien to the slow-changing dinosaurs.

What struck Darwin most on his expedition was the force of change, the fact that not only did the tortoises of the Galapagos archipelago differ from anything on the American mainland, but also from one island to the other: 'It is the circumstance that several of the islands possess their own species of tortoise, mocking-thrush, finches and numerous plants . . . that strikes me with wonder.'[24]

In Galapagos, wondering why there was diversity within species helped Darwin to formulate his theory of evolution, the slow process of change in which individuals survive by adapting to their environments, what the evolutionary philosopher Herbert Spencer (1820–1903) called the Survival

Two distinct Galapagos sub-species: domed (*left*) and Saddleback (*right*). Of the original fourteen sub-species three are now extinct.

of the Fittest. Expounded in *On the Origin of Species by Means of Natural Selection; or, The Preservation of Favoured Races in the Struggle for Life* (1859), Darwin's views were counter to the prevailing literal, creationist interpretation of the Book of Genesis and radically altered man's understanding of his place in the scheme of things. Tortoises thus had their role from the mid-nineteenth century in upsetting received scientific

and religious ideas. On those grounds alone the creature is
entitled to a reputation for possessing ancient wisdom of
enduring significance. At the beginning of the twenty-first
century the controversy it helped to prompt has not ceased,
since it is kept alive by Bible fundamentalists in the American
Mid-West and Deep South, notably in the states of Kansas
and Alabama.

A spur-thighed or 'Greek' tortoise in an 1880s French scientific illustration. *Testudo graeca* is common in countries bordering the Mediterranean.

Diversity among the creatures is even more evident internationally. There are some 250 species of tortoises, turtles and terrapins, the latter being a freshwater group. Most of them are aquatic or amphibian, only some 50 of the 250 being land tortoises. Experts disagree on exactly how many genera and species there are. They are named for various reasons, an obvious one being physical characteristics such as angulated, elongated, flat-shelled, geometric, impressed, leopard, parrot-beaked, radiated, red- or yellow-footed, speckled, spur-thighed and tent. Some were named after their discoverers or identifiers such as Bell (1828), Gray (1863), Hermann (1789) and Kleinmann (1883). Often such surnames are used only in the scientific name, the readily understood description being more commonly used. A third type of name is provenance, for example Burmese or Indian star, Central Asian, desert, Karroo Cape, Texas or Travancore.

Wherever they occur, tortoises have adapted to their various natural environments around the world. They were well distributed over the warmer parts of the earth's surface, ubiquitous in all temperate and tropical areas except Australia and Polynesia. The original ones, appearing around 225 million years ago in the Mesozoic Era, would have been inhabitants of Pangaea, the super-continent that existed until about 200 million years ago. The Mesozoic Era was a time of heightened global tectonic activity, during which Pangaea split and resplit into the continents and islands recognized on maps today.

In geological time, continental drift took the land creatures to different environments in which they would develop distinct characteristics. For instance, during the Lower Cretaceous period, when iguanodons were flourishing with tortoises in what is now Belgium, that territory was much further south, at a latitude of about $35°$ North with a subtropical climate. Today it is $50°$ North. It may be that the dinosaurs were unable to cope with the migration of the continents into different climatic zones with much cooler conditions and became extinct. Tortoises survived because they adapted to their often hostile environments, but in acting defensively they boxed themselves into an evolutionary dead end. Myths about them, however, continued to grow.

2 Myths and Symbols

An anecdote about the structure of our universe opens Stephen Hawking's *A Brief History of Time* (1988):

> A well-known scientist (some say it was Bertrand Russell) once gave a public lecture on astronomy. He described how the earth orbits round the sun and how the sun, in turn, orbits around the centre of a vast collection of stars called our galaxy. At the end of the lecture, a little old lady at the back of the room got up and said: 'What you have told us is rubbish. The world is really a flat plate supported on the back of a giant tortoise.' The scientist gave a superior smile before replying, 'What is the tortoise standing on?' 'You're very clever young man, very clever,' said the old lady. 'But it's turtles all the way down.'

The reference to turtles may be confusing to readers outside the USA; Americans often use the term to include tortoises. There are many versions of the 'turtles all the way down' story. One suggestion is that the lecturer early in the twentieth century at Harvard was William James, the philosopher and elder brother of the novelist Henry James.

The whole idea of a chthonian creature is imaginative but

impractical. In the eighteenth century, according to the historian Edward Gibbon, Mr Malthus observed that a tortoise supporting the earth posed a problem: 'This explanation only removes the difficulty a little farther off. It makes the earth rest upon a tortoise, but does not tell us on what the tortoise rests.'[1] Looking back to the later years of the nineteenth century, when he was a young man, George Bernard Shaw (1856–1950) said in the preface to his play of 1921, *Back to Methuselah*: 'In those days . . . we were invited to pity the delusion of certain heathens who held that the world is supported by an elephant who is supported by a tortoise . . . We refuted these orientals by asking triumphantly what the tortoise stands on?'

The old lady who challenged the lecturer could point to oriental creation beliefs long and widely held. Not mythical, the creature was certainly mythogenic. In Chinese myth, at the

P'an Ku, 'the Chinese Adam', the first being brought into existence by cosmological evolution, was the legendary great architect of the universe. Over 18,000 years, with chisel, mallet and the divine creatures – dragon, phoenix and tortoise – at his right hand, he fashioned huge masses of granite floating aimlessly in space.

beginning of creation Gong Gong, god of water, quarrelled with Zhu Rong, god of fire. Gong Gong, in some versions the son of Zhu Rong, was half reptile/half man, having a human head with red hair on the body of a serpent. Envying the power of Zhu Rong, benevolent lord of the cosmos, Gong Gong tried to overthrow him but was unsuccessful. In frustrated rage he hurled himself against Imperfect Mountain in the north-west, one of the four rock pillars that supported the world. Being immortal, Gong Gong was unhurt but he shattered the mountain, leaving a hole in the sky that caused the world to tilt, creating floods and the other natural disasters that China is subject to. The creator goddess Nü Gua came to the rescue by filling the hole in the sky, propping it up with the four legs of a giant, immortal tortoise and shoring up all the breached river banks. Similarly, the turbulent Isles of the Immortals finally came to rest only when the tortoises intervened, took charge of them and set them on their backs.[2]

The tortoise both supports the world, its four feet being the four corners of the earth, and is a model of the world itself.[3] It represents the Great Triad, the sky the dome of its back, the earth its lower shell and the atmosphere its body in between.[4] Chinese emperors recognized its significance by having the base of their tombs carved in the shape of a tortoise. Its four stumpy legs are set firmly on the ground, like the pillars of a temple. In Japan, it has a similar Atlas-like role, holding up the Cosmic Mountain and the home of the Sennin, the Genii or Immortals of Taoist philosophy.[5] A creation myth of the Aryan people who settled in India in the middle years of the second millennium BC was that the world was formed from a cosmic egg. The creator Brahma or Prajapati squeezed the egg and its contents emerged to form a tortoise shape, Kurma, the equivalent of the Great Triad in Chinese mythology.[6]

Hindu myth is based on a trinity of powers: Brahma, the creator; Vishnu, the preserver; and Shiva, the destroyer. During the creation, when the powers were at war, *amrita*, the cream of the primordial milk ocean, was lost, along with other heavenly treasures, threatening the continued existence of the universe. Vishnu, who had the ability to manifest himself in various forms or avatars, descended as Kurma the tortoise. He advised using Mount Mandara as a paddle and the great serpent Vasuki as a rope to churn the Ocean of Milk until the treasures appeared. In this way the gods recovered *amrita*, the wishing cow Surabhi, the elephant Airavata and many wonderful jewels and other objects. In his incarnation as a tortoise Vishnu-Kurma stayed under-water throughout the operation, holding up Mount Mandara so that it would not sink under its own weight. To this day Kurma is still regarded as underpinning India.[7]

The final avatar of Vishnu, Kalkin, will appear when virtue and religion have gone and the world is under the command of unjust men. Kalkin, mounted on a white horse and brandishing a mighty sword, will come to set the world to rights, overcoming the unjust and inaugurating a golden age. In some versions of the myth Kalkin's white horse will strike the earth with its right foot, dislodging the tortoise that supports the world and tumbling him into the ocean. The way will then be clear for the gods to restore the earth to its primeval purity.[8] As an incarnation of Vishnu, the tortoise also appears in Tibetan mythology. Its green face represents either generation or regeneration as the creature emerges from the primordial waters bearing the earth upon its back.[9]

Yet another Indian version has Chukwa the tortoise supporting the elephant Maha-pudma, which in turn supports the world.[10] Together the female lunar tortoise, which governs

This 1780s painting from Lucknow shows Kurma, the tortoise incarnation of Vishnu, supporting Mount Mandara all the while it is being used as a churning stick in the Ocean of Milk.

the waters, and the male solar elephant stand for the two creative powers. These myths were translated into ancient maps in which India was shown as tortoise-shaped. Its head faced east, its tail west, and its front flippers north and south. Sometimes the country appeared as a continent floating on a tortoise's back in the centre of a cosmic ocean with all the other known countries and the stars swimming round it. During the construction of the northern altar, representing the universe, a live tortoise was placed in the first layer of bricks. In the central part of a temple, the creature was both the source of all things and a sure base.[11]

For the Mongols of Central Asia, a golden tortoise supported the mountain at the centre of the universe.[12] In Balinese cosmology the cosmic serpent Antaboga created through meditation the cosmic turtle Bedawang. Upon Bedawang rested two coiled snakes, the foundations of the earth, and the Black Stone, the cover of the underworld.[13]

The concept of the tortoise upholding the world is not confined to the Orient. It occurs in Amerindian traditions, for example among the Huron. According to the Sioux, the world is a huge tortoise floating on the waters. Other versions have the tortoise saving people from the Flood and then bearing the new earth on its back, or the cosmic tree growing out of its back.[14] The North American term 'turtle' survives in place names, especially in the Mid-West. In Canada, for instance, there are Turtle Mountain in Manitoba, Turtleford in Saskatchewan and Lac à la Tortue in Québec. In the USA there are Turtle Hill (in the Indian language *Keya Paha*) near Northfield, Minnesota, Turtle Lake in North Dakota, Wisconsin and Minnesota, which also has a Turtle River. North Dakota has the Turtle Mountain Indian Reservation. Turtle Creek occurs in Ohio, Pennsylvania and West Virginia. Further south there is a

Turtletown in Tennessee, Tortugas in Florida and a Turtle Bayou in Texas. Mexico has Bahia Tortugas.

References occur in the Mayan civilization of Yucatán. Among tribes living within the great bend of the Niger River in West Africa the tortoise is also regarded as a representative of the universe.[15] Thus in several places the tortoise figures high in the hierarchy of creation. Why should it be associated with something as fundamental as the beginning of the universe?

There is the obvious point that the creature was well established for more than 200 million years before man came on the scene. Early man was perplexed by the mystery of creation and, being ancient and self-contained in appearance, the tortoise offered a ready answer. It gave the impression of harbouring fundamental truths, and it was easy to imagine it as present at the creation and with a role in the process. That the same basic myth should occur in territories far apart is not surprising.

This still does not explain why, across widely separated cultures, early man should believe in similar basic myths of creation. Geological theories about the breakup of Pangaea, the continental drift of tectonic plates proposed in the twentieth century, would have been unknown to him. We are not dealing with legends, which have a basis in fact. It would seem that cosmic myths of the tortoise had their origin in eastern Asia, where they were most firmly and widely held. From there *Homo sapiens* could well have taken them across the Beringia land-bridge into North America from the first migrations, which started at least around 13,000 BC. In a grand but probably gradual sweep, an arc of an idea stretched from East Asia right down eventually to Central America. The myth was diffused through the migration of peoples; in its travels the story was simplified and distorted like a message being whispered around a circle, the fundamental idea being locally adapted.

But how to account for the appearance in West Africa? Serendipity is a simple explanation. On closer examination the myth is akin to the basic local culture. For instance, among one of the peoples there, the Dogon, families commonly own a tortoise, which is regarded as next to the head of the family, receiving the first food and water of the day when the head is absent.[16] The widespread prevalence of similar myths also supports the Jungian psychology theory of their origin: that people unconsciously form the same mythic symbols. Like the serpent and the sphinx, the tortoise is an archetype in the collective unconscious of the human race. Just like the tortoise, the collective unconscious is a repository of ancient wisdom. The German philosopher Friedrich Wilhelm Nietzsche (1844–1900), however, a searcher for big ideas like those of the ancient Greek thinkers, regarded contemporary philosophy as 'the gospel of the tortoise', little more than plodding around the ruins of great thoughts.[17]

Examples of the collective unconscious are recurring associations of the moon and regeneration. In Chinese myth, re-generation comes from the fertile primordial waters, associated with phases of the moon. According to a Bangladeshi tribe, the tortoise is a demiurge entrusted by the all-powerful sun and husband of the moon with the mission of rescuing the earth from the bottom of the sea. The Mayan moon-god has a tortoise as a breastplate. Links were made between the thirteen scutes on the upper part of a tortoise carapace and the identical number of lunar months. From the moon it was a short step to linking with other heavenly bodies, the stars. In Yucatec, Orion's shield is known as the tortoise.[18] The Mayan system of three calendars was sometimes depicted as a segmented wheel, and tortoises from their form were a natural symbol of the passing of time. Similarly, the motifs are associated with rituals performed at certain times.

In China's Forbidden City, from 1421 the Imperial Palace of the Ming and Qing dynasties, the bronze tortoise is one of the four celestial creatures on view.

Whereas myths associated with the tortoise have been fairly consistent, its attributes have been very different. Because of its antiquity it is not one symbol but many, some interconnected, an association of ideas. Others reflect cultural diversity, different perceptions within the same geographical area. Throughout its long history the tortoise has lived in an *Alice Through the Looking-Glass* world: "'When *I* use a word,' Humpty Dumpty said in a rather scornful tone, 'it means just what I choose it to mean – neither more nor less.'" As we shall see, Humpty Dumpty was probably a 'tortoise'.

A natural attribute is longevity, shared in China with the crane. Longevity is a sign of endurance; so the tortoise is a sound foundation for a building. It is said that the wooden columns of the Temple of Heaven, built in Beijing in 1420, were originally set on live tortoises, since the animals were believed to be able to live for 3,000 years without food and air, and have the power to preserve wood from decay. A card with the words *loe-ling*, meaning the great age of the tortoise, was a way of

wishing somebody 'Many happy returns'. In *The Religious System of China* (1892–1910), J. J. M. de Groot notes:

> Among the hairpins provided for a woman's burial is almost always one which is adorned with small silver figures of a stag, a tortoise, a peach and a crane. These being emblems of longevity, it is supposed that the pin which is decorated with them will absorb some of their life-giving power and communicate it to the woman in whose hair it is ultimately to be fastened.[19]

The tortoise also represented strength and endurance as the Black Warrior. With the dragon, on banners carried by the imperial army, it was a symbol of indestructibility since both

The stone tortoise in the Buddha Temple in Hai Chuang Park, Guangzhou province, carries on its back a serpent, a creature of power that gave birth to the emperors of China. Together the serpent and the tortoise were a guard against evil forces.

Another version in Wong Tai Sin Temple, Guangzhou. A shepherd boy become a god, Wong Tai Sin created an immortal drug and is seen as a god of healing.

creatures could survive a fight. The dragon was unable to crush the tortoise and the tortoise could not reach the dragon. Later, within the Taoist pantheon, the Black Warrior became the Perfected Warrior in human form. As such, along with the Great Wall, he was the protector of the state and the throne against invaders from Central Asia.[20]

On amulets, minted as early as the Han dynasty (202 BC–220 AD), tortoises were a symbol to ward off evil spirits and unpropitious influences. Amulets were sometimes put under the bed of newly married couples, tied on wrists soon after birth, sewn on the headdress of a child. Placed under the door-sill or kitchen furnace when built, their purpose was to secure good luck for the builder or the family occupying the house.

One of the notable characteristics is perseverance. Tortoises do not give up easily. This is particularly evident in males, distinguished from females by their concave under-shells, wanting to mount and mate. They will pursue females, knocking against them to put them off their stride and snapping at their legs to slow them down. When Mika Hakkinen, the Finnish racing driver, became Formula One World Champion in 1998 he stated that the tortoise was his favourite animal, not because of its speed but for its persistence. Hakkinen went on to become World Champion again in 1999, by a whisker in the last race of the season.

The physical as opposed to the mythical attributes of tortoises are fewer and consistent. A tortoise is a tortoise is a tortoise. What has varied over the centuries, depending on the culture at a particular place and time, are human attitudes towards the creatures.

Although the myth of Zhu Rong and Gong Gong is a victory of fire over water, the tortoise, with the dragon, phoenix and *ky-lin*, is one of the Four Spiritually Endowed Creatures. It represents the watery element, the passive, feminine, negative *yin* principle of the two opposing forces in the universe.[21] In Taoism and Confucianism it is shown as the dark tadpole-like half of a circle, interlocking with the masculine bright half.

The Yuan dynasty (1260–1368) song *Dan Bian Duo Su* mocks Li Yuanji, son of the T'ang emperor Tai-zong, for behaving like a tortoise and shirking danger. This has its origin in the similarity of a tortoise's head to a penis, emerging as an erection and retracting in detumescence. At the time weak and cowardly husbands who let their wives carry on affairs were looked upon as tortoises that dared not face the fact. That term for cuckolds has endured, mainly in northern China; in the south, the description is more likely to be used for someone overcharging a customer. It is also applied to pimps who brush aside the intercourse that supports them.[22]

J. J. M. de Groot records a late nineteenth-century occasion when the appearance of the creature was unwelcome:

> Some thirty years ago the wise men of Shanghai were much exercised to discover the cause of a local rebellion. On careful enquiry they ascertained that the rebellion was due to the shape of a large new temple which had most unfortunately been built in the shape of a tortoise, an animal of the very worst character. The difficulty was serious, the danger was pressing; for to pull down the temple would have been impious, and to let it stand as it was would be to court a succession of similar or worse disasters. However, the genius of the local professors of geomancy, rising to the occasion, triumphantly surmounted the difficulty and obviated the danger. By filling up two wells, which represented the eyes of the tortoise, they at once blinded that disreputable animal and rendered him incapable of doing further mischief.[23]

In modern Chinese society, 'tortoise egg' or 'grandson of a tortoise' is a term of abuse. 'Tortoise hair' describes a hedger or waffler unwilling to stick his neck out for anything. In Taiwan the expression for losing your shirt translates literally as 'knocking tortoises'. The association with bad luck is not good news for gamblers. Hence, as the popularity of numbers games has risen, so the demand for cakes depicting tortoises has fallen. In the past they were used as offerings at temple festivals or big family events such as weddings and major birthdays.

Opposed attributes exist within a culture and between cultures. Kumpira, the Japanese god of seafaring men, similarly had a tortoise as his protective emblem against the elements. The emblem also occurs on the guards of samurai swords. Withdrawing into its shell, though, was a sign of cowardice, a refusal to confront a situation head-on.[24] To Hindus, on the other hand, this indicated turning away from the world and into oneself, a spiritual concentration, a return to the primal state.[25]

From long life the association spread to the ideas of wisdom and immortality. In the South-East Asian kingdom of Annam, now Vietnam, a Golden Tortoise living under a waterfall was a hermit sage consulted by the king in times of need.[26] According to legend, in medieval Vietnam a tortoise was close to the gods. In the mid-fifteenth century, when the great Vietnamese hero Le Loi was out in a sampan fishing, he netted a gleaming magical sword that he then used to drive the Chinese out of his country. After ten years of successful campaigning, returning as Emperor Le Tai To, he wanted to thank the spirit of the lake. As he made ready his sacrifice there was a roll of thunder, the sword flew out of its scabbard and was caught in the mouth of a giant golden tortoise swimming on the surface. It was an emissary of the gods, sent to reclaim the heaven-sent weapon. The event gave its name to the lake in the heart of the capital, Hanoi, Hoan Kiem Lake, Lake of the Restored Sword. On an islet in the middle of the lake a three-tiered pavilion known as the Tortoise Tower or Pagoda commemorates the event, and the Tower is often used as the emblem of Hanoi. In Vietnamese the word for tortoise and turtle is the same. Large turtles still swim in the lake and one, heavily varnished, is preserved on a second island.

A golden tortoise also occurs in the legend of Manjushri, the Bodhisattva or future Buddha of wisdom, who originally taught the meanings of astrological treatises to mankind. When man neglected them in favour of other thoughts Manjushri reabsorbed the teachings, which became his hidden mind treasure. From his mind he projected a golden tortoise, causing it to arise from the primal ocean. Firing a golden arrow from his bow, he made the tortoise roll over on to its back so that he could write the astrological teachings on its under-shell. These foretell man's destinies, but the array of numbers and symbols has to be interpreted.

The *Bhagavad Gita* ('Song of the Blessed'), the supreme religious work of Hinduism, a philosophical Sanskrit poem written about 300 BC, cites the tortoise as an example to be followed:

> The tortoise brings up its offspring simply by meditation. The eggs of the tortoise are laid on land, and the tortoise meditates on the eggs while in the water. Similarly, the devotee of Krishna consciousness, although far away from the Lord's abode, can elevate himself to that abode simply by thinking of Him constantly – by engagement in Krishna consciousness.[27]

In another version, Kasyapa, the Sanskrit word for tortoise, was the husband of Daksha's thirteen daughters, the lunar months. By them he was the father of all creatures great and small. In paintings and sculpture he is depicted as the primordial tortoise with a never-ending clutch of eggs.

In Philippine mythology the tortoise's ability to move its head in and out of its shell is a bringer of good fortune. A fisherman, Yusup, caught a white tortoise, which he called Notu. When Yusup went fishing, Notu in the bow of the boat looked steadily in one direction until he came to a good fishing ground, when he would draw his head in. One day Notu guided Yusup due east for three days and nights. Suddenly a huge sea monster reared up, ordered Yusup to make for an island and, by blowing into his sails, pushed him into a bay. On the beach was a palace belonging to the monster, in fact a bewitched prince. He could be released if Yusup could fish up a magic ring that the prince had lost. With his unerring sense of where to look, the tortoise guided his master to it and Yusup was well rewarded.[28]

To some, the virtue of endurance is a sign of obstinacy. Able to appear and disappear, the tortoise can be regarded as a trickster. One of the Middle Eastern folk tales with which Scheherazade entertained the Sultan for *The Thousand and One Nights* to prevent her being strangled at daybreak was 'The Prince and the Tortoise'. Having the most outstanding qualities of the Sultan's three sons, Prince Muhammed seemed to be the least fortunate when it came to finding the wife for whom he had been destined. Whereas his brothers' arrows fell upon the houses of noble maidens, Muhammed's landed on the home of a lonely tortoise. Nevertheless, against his father's wishes, the prince was determined to fulfil his destiny. Even when his father

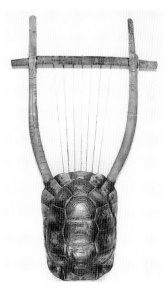

An Ancient Greek wooden lyre (c. 300 BC) with tortoise shell soundbox restored from remains. In his 1757 ode, *The Progress of Poesy,* Thomas Gray called the Aeolian lyre 'Enchanting shell!'

became ill and his sons decided that their wives should care for him, Muhammed retained confidence in his reptile wife. The tortoise tricked her sisters-in-law into seasoning the Sultan's food with mice, rat, hen and pigeon droppings, claiming that they were the finest ingredients. Their smell revolted the Sultan, who naturally preferred the tortoise's cuisine, which restored his health. At the feast to celebrate, the tortoise again tricked her sisters-in-law into arriving on a goat and a goose, making a mockery of the Sultan's rank. Meanwhile, the tortoise transformed herself into a comely maiden, who performed magical feats at the feast. So impressed was the Sultan that he bequeathed his entire kingdom to Muhammed, who became the father of many children.[29]

In cultures not geographically far apart there were widely differing views. For example, in Mexico among the Aztecs the tortoise was a symbol of cowardice and boastfulness, hard outside and soft inside.[30] To the Mayans, the pre-Columbian civilization of Central America, the animal was an expression of hope for a long life beyond rebirth.[31]

In Graeco-Roman mythology, the goddess of fertility, Aphrodite / Venus, born of the sea, is a prime example of the feminine power of water and has the tortoise as her emblem Similarly, Hermes / Mercury is associated with fertility. A cunning child, he caught a large tortoise, cleaned the shell, stretched cowhide over the opening to make a sound-chest, mounted it on a frame of antelope horns and wood, strung it with cow-gut from cattle that he had stolen from Apollo, god of music, and thus invented the lyre.[32] In the words of Percy Bysshe Shelley (1792–1822),

When he had wrought the lovely instrument,
He tried the chords, and made division meet,

This woodcut from the *Hypnerotomachia Poliphili* (1499) depicts a woman holding a tortoise in one hand and a pair of wings in the other, a contrast of the earthly and the heavenly. Hermeticists have interpreted them as two aspects of Hermes, the tortoise being the creature that he transformed into a lyre. By extension, it became a symbol of the raw material of the art of alchemy.

Preluding with the plectrum, and there went
Up from beneath his hand a tumult sweet
Of mighty sounds.[33]

Producing sounds never before heard, the instrument enchanted Apollo, who willingly allowed Hermes to keep his stolen cows in exchange. Hermes, whose lyre had three, perhaps four strings, was credited with inventing the musical scale. His innovation is believed to be the basis of a Roman stone sculpture with Hellenic influences dating from 130–100 BC and depicting a youth with a tortoise under his arm. It was discovered in 1968 at Genainville in the department of Val d'Oise, north of Paris.

According to the myth, Apollo later gave a lyre to Orpheus, son of Calliope, the muse of heroic epic. So sweet was the playing of Orpheus that his lyre was able to charm wild beasts and move rocks and trees. The greatest singer and musician of ancient Greece, he was even able, when he descended into Hades to recover his wife, Eurydice, to charm the three-headed guard dog, Cerberus, and make the damned forget their tortures.

The tortoise was sacred to Hermes' son, Pan, another fertility god, and killing it was forbidden. As the art critic John Ruskin (1819–1900) put it in his lecture of 1870, 'The Tortoise of Aegina': 'Remember only that the tortoise shell, as part of the lyre, whether of Hermes or Orpheus, signifies the measured Harmony and spheric order of life.'[34] Amazonian Indians regard the tortoise as a representation of the vagina, and a tortoise shell sealed at one end with wax becomes a musical instrument played at some of their initiation ceremonies.[35]

In West Africa it embodies the female principle and features widely in fertility rites. Among the Yoruba of Western Nigeria the tortoise is depicted in folk tales as a trickster, sometimes too cunning for his own good. For instance, in one tale he steals from the gods a calabash, a fruit in the form of a gourd, containing all the wisdom in the world. To carry it home he takes the easy way and hangs it round his neck. When he is confronted with a tree trunk across his path the calabash proves to be a further obstacle. It gets in his way and, although he is a good climber, he cannot get over the trunk. In his frustration he does not think of carrying the fruit on his back. Instead he smashes it, thus scattering wisdom in fragments all over the world forever. Some may have landed in Cameroon, where, in one tribe, suspects sat on a tortoise stool, or stool of judgement, to prevent them lying when answering charges levelled against them.[36]

In another Nigerian folk tale, *The Hippopotamus and the Tortoise*, the tortoise again shows his artfulness. On the pretext that they could not guess his name, known only to his seven fat wives, the hippopotamus refused people food at his table. Before the people left, the tortoise asked the hippopotamus what he would do if somebody was able to reveal his name at the next feast. The hippopotamus replied that in shame he and his seven wives would forsake the land and live in water, where the tortoise knew they went morning and evening to bathe and drink. One day the tortoise half buried himself in a hole that he had dug in the path of two lagging wives. One of the wives barked her foot on the tortoise's shell and immediately cried out: 'O Isantim, my husband, I've hurt my foot.' At the next feast the tortoise revealed the name to the delight of the people, who were able to share the tasty food and palm wine with their host. Fulfilling his pledge, the hippopotamus and his seven wives then went down to the river, where they have lived ever since, only coming ashore to feed at night. Just so.[37]

For the inhabitants of Calabar in West Africa, the creature could be a man's external soul, the death or injury of which necessarily entailed the death or injury of the man. Sickness was a sign that his bush soul was angry, and the offending spirit had to be placated with an offering to the place where the animal was last seen. If the bush soul was appeased, the patient recovered; if not he died.

In another African folk tale, the tortoise plays a leading role against two larger animals, an elephant and a hippopotamus. He wants to be regarded as their equal but they say he is too small to be anything like. A trickster, he challenges them both to a tug of war and succeeds in pitting them against one another.

They have to acknowledge that he is their equal. Listeners to this dilemma or judgement tale may take the view expressed in George Orwell's satire *Animal Farm* (1946): 'All animals are equal but some animals are more equal than others.'

Naturally the tortoise has acquired superstitions, some of which the anthropologist and folklorist Sir James Frazer included in *The Golden Bough* (1890–1915):

> Animals are often employed as a vehicle for carrying away or transferring evil . . . In some parts of Algeria people think that typhoid fever can be cured by taking a tortoise, putting it on its back in the road and covering it with a pot. The patient recovers, but whoever upsets the pot catches the fever.[38]

A seventeenth-century Dutch emblem of morality.

A common use was in homeopathic or imitative magic:

When the Galla [the Galla are a North African people] sees a tortoise, he will take off his sandals and step on it, believing that the soles of his feet are thereby made hard and strong like the shell of the animal.[39]

Cherokee ball-players . . . apply land tortoises to their legs in the hope of making them as thick and strong as the legs of these animals.[40]

One superstition dates from 1665:

The Caribs abstained from the flesh of pigs lest it should cause them to have small eyes like pigs; and they refused to partake of tortoises from a fear that if they did they would become heavy and stupid like the animal.[41]

To Calvinist Christians, the tortoise can represent modesty in marriage, women living in the seclusion of the home. The contrast between worldly materialism and domestic bliss was particularly brought out in the Netherlands in the seventeenth century. In *Wtnementheit des Vrouwelijke Geslachts* (On the Excellence of the Female Sex), Johan van Beverwijck depicted the ideal wife not as a figure standing on top of the world but on a tortoise. Still bearing a torch in her left hand, she has resolved the conflict between the attractions of the wider world and the call to homely duties by the compromise of a mobile home. Behind her Adam delves in the garden while Eve spins within the cottage. The tortoise was adopted as an emblem of morality. If a wife had to leave home then she should conduct herself as though she had never left it.

The notion was the foundation of an early eighteenth-century Central European church dedicated to the Virgin Mary, the ideal chaste wife. Designed by the architect Jan Blazej Santini in the shape of a tortoise, it was built in the years 1730–34 in Obyčtov, Bohemia. The body of the church is an oval, with chapels in the 'legs', the 'head' facing east and the 'tail' west.[42]

In early Christian art, though, the tortoise is a sign of evil in contrast to the cock of vigilance. Whereas the tortoise hides in its shell, a sign of darkness and ignorance, the cock crows in the morning as it becomes light and represents the dawn of enlightenment. For instance, inside the west door and in the crypt of the basilica at Aquileia in north-east Italy there are colourful mosaics including panels of a cock fighting a tortoise. The mosaics, one of the most remarkable early Christian monuments in Italy, were laid down soon after 313 AD during the time of the first patriarch, Theodore. St Jerome (c. 342–420), biblical scholar and the most learned of the Latin Fathers, argued that tortoises moved slowly because they were burdened with the weight of sin. Association of the creature with

By the 17th century tortoises were considered fit artistic subjects in their own right, as in this painting, *The Five Senses* (also called *Still-Life with Musical Instruments*) of 1623 by Dutch artist Pieter Claesz. The tortoise is present as the origin of music.

Medieval manuscripts deigned to include tortoises as illustrations, even though in the contemporary Christian view the creature was a symbol of Darkness. Both of these *c.* 1350 column miniatures are from Jacob van Maerlant, *Der Naturen Bloeme*, Flanders. (*above*) An 'Accipender' tortoise; (*below*) a 'Tortuca' tortoise.

evil probably derives from Leviticus 11: 29: 'These also shall be unclean unto you among the creeping things that creep upon the earth; the weasel, and the mouse, and the tortoise after his kind.'

The view persisted. In his allegorical and religious scenes, for instance *The Concert in the Egg*, the Netherlandish painter Hieronymus Bosch (*c.* 1450–1516) gave the creatures no prominence. When the late Renaissance artist of the Venetian school Jacopo da Bassano (1510–1592) came to paint Adam with animals (*c.* 1590; now Prado, Madrid), the pair of tortoises were consigned to deep gloom at the foot of his large horizontal canvas.

In one medieval Italian city, Siena, the tortoise had a place of honour as an emblem of one of the original 22 *contrade*, the individual quarters that from the early fourteenth century were each capable of raising two military units. Each *contrada*, generally denoted by an animal, developed under a governing council a system of collective civil life based on its church and social centre. Citizen loyalty is to the *contrada*, and streets and alleys in its quarter are identified with its emblem. Today the seventeen surviving *contrade* are in three groups: the *Tartuca* (tortoise) belonging in the south-west corner of the city with the eagle, snail, wave, panther and forest. The *Tartuca*, distinguished by its blue and yellow banner, is under the patronage of St Anthony of Padua, an early thirteenth-century Franciscan friar, 'hammer of heretics' and a Doctor of the Church, in whose honour the inhabitants of the *Tartuca* built a church in 1684. Since the Middle Ages the *contrade* have competed in the *Palio*, the horse race with the prize of a banner that, on a Christian feast day, is more a trial of trickery by the riders than a test of equestrian speed. On this occasion the colourful *contrade* banners and apparel, reminiscent of their military origin, are well displayed.[43]

An ensign in the colourful costume of the tortoise *contrada*. He demonstrates his acrobatic skill by swinging the flag to the sound of rolling drums.

According to a Persian proverb, 'contempt penetrates even the shell of the tortoise'. In the Middle Ages, when the Ottoman Empire was expanding at the expense of Byzantium, the largely Greek remnant of what had been the Roman Empire, there was a similar lowly view, footnoted by Edward Gibbon (1737–1794) in his *Decline and Fall of the Roman Empire*: 'The opprobrious

name which the Turks bestow on infidels is expressed by Ducas . . . The term is derived by Ducange (Gloss. Graec tom. i. p. 530) . . . in vulgar Greek, a tortoise, as denoting a retrograde motion from the faith.'[44]

On the other hand, to the American agnostic Robert G. Ingersoll (1833–1899) praising Thomas Paine, there was 'the tortoise Truth that beats the rabbit Lie in the long run'.[45] The horror novelist Stephen King portrayed it as morally neutral, apart from the conflict. He chose the primeval creature – 'I made the universe, but don't blame me for it' – as the unwilling creator of the eternal, constantly metamorphosing evil It in his blockbuster novel *It* (1986).

Myths in their variety have endured into modern times as beliefs, stories and entertainment. It was not just the old lady

The notion of the tortoise holding up the world is carried through into support for two obelisks in Piazza Santa Maria Novella, Florence. The two obelisks, set up in 1608, are used as turning posts in the annual chariot race, Palio dei Cocchi. Giambologna (1529-1608), a Flemish sculptor influenced by Michelangelo, designed the bronze tortoises.

A tortoise bears the weight of a column at Gaudí's Art Nouveau cathedral, Sagrada Familia, in Barcelona.

berating the lecturer on his theory of the universe who accepted the tortoise as a foundation. The symbolism was perpetuated in Italian piazza monuments. In the thirteenth-century Piazza Santa Maria Novella in Florence, two obelisks resting on bronze tortoises by the Flemish sculptor Giambologna were set up in 1608 as turning posts in the annual chariot race. The graceful Fontana delle Tartarughe (1584) in the Piazza Mattei, Rome, was restored perhaps by Gianlorenzo Bernini in 1658, when the tortoises were added. At the base of the tree of life in Antonio Gaudí's great Art Nouveau church in Barcelona, the Sagrada Familia (begun 1882), is a carved tortoise. The notion is the basis of a modern fantasy, *The Colour of Magic* (1983), the first volume of Terry Pratchett's Discworld (as opposed to Roundworld) series of novels, the prologue of which is:

In a distant and second-hand set of dimensions, in an astral plane that was never meant to fly, the curling star-mists waver and part . . . See . . . Great A'Tuin the Turtle comes, swimming slowly through the interstellar gulf, hydrogen frost on his ponderous limbs, his huge and ancient shell pocked with meteor craters. Through sea-sized eyes that are crusted with rheum and asteroid dust He stares fixedly at the Destination.

In a brain bigger than a city, with geological slow-ness, He thinks only of the Weight. Most of the weight is of course accounted for by Berilia, Tubul, Great T'Phon and Jerakeen, the four giant elephants upon whose broad and star-tanned shoulders the disc of the World rests, garlanded by the long waterfall at its vast circum-ference and domed by the baby-blue vault of Heaven.

In a later volume, *Small Gods* (1992), the talking tortoise is soon revealed to be the Great God Om, a Brahmin name used by modern occultists to signify spiritual essence or absolute goodness and truth.

By his 54th birthday in 2002, Terry Pratchett had produced 26 novels in the Discworld series. A blend of fantasy, humour and satire imaginatively set among witches, wizards, dwarves and elves, the books appeal to readers of all ages. Asked where his inspiration came from, *The Guardian* reported that Pratchett acknowledged that Discworld 'belonged to world mythology, but I stole it and ran away before the alarms went off.'

When Paul Manning, the English interpreter in Michael Frayn's novel *The Russian Interpreter* (1966), remarks 'It's the circumstances around me that make me discontented', his Russian girl friend Katerina replies: 'The circumstances around you are part of you. People carry their lives about with them like tortoises carry their shells.' Manning found the grave aphorism a solace.[46]

In Nina Bawden's novel *Tortoise by Candlelight* (1963), Emmie, aged 14, is the mainstay of the home in the absence of her grandmother, who dies; the weakness of her drunken father; her older sister getting herself into trouble with her boyfriend; the misdemeanours of her 8-year-old brother, Oliver, a liar and a thief who keeps two tortoises in his bedroom. Like the tortoise holding up the world, Emmie provides a stable base, guiding the family through its troubles, which she sees as only a passing phase. Like time, the tortoise is enduring, occurring for instance in Salman Rushdie's novel *Midnight's Children* (1981), where with a touch of magic realism the narrator in his fevered imagination is trying to determine his identity: 'I am perhaps the Elephant. Who, like Sin the moon, controls the waters, bringing the gift of rain . . . whose mother was Ira, queen consort of Kashyap, the Old Tortoise Man, lord and progenitor of all creatures on the earth.'[47]

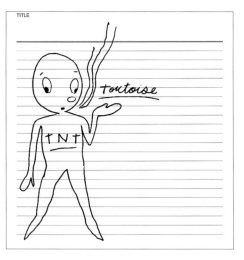

The sleeve of a Tortoise band CD.

The association of the tortoise and music continues. In his posthumously published *Common-place Book* (1849), the writer Robert Southey noted: 'In Yucatán they made a musical instrument of the tortoise-shell preserved whole.'[48] Uncaring tourists can still buy such crude instruments as souvenirs. Appropriately, descendants of the lyre – guitars, bass and lap steel – are feature instruments played in relaxed style by the Chicago rock band Tortoise. Its distinctive style of music without words has given rise to the description 'Tortesian'. Again appropriately, the music critic Patrick Gough drew on ancient Greek classics to define the sound:

Tortoise's music has an epic quality to it that's paradoxically grand yet understated at the same time. Since I used the word 'epic', I'll make a literary analogy. The members of Tortoise all played punk rock at some point, but now play a more toned-down, complex kind of music. Kind of like the progression in tone from Homer's *Iliad* to the *Odyssey*. In the *Iliad*, the Greek warriors were fired up and angry; but in the *Odyssey*, after the Trojan War – approaching middle age – the men became more reflective, calm, and dignified, but no less passionate. Since those are themes most of us past a certain age can recognize, Tortoise's humble instrumental lines have become the soundtrack of a generation of punk rockers trying to gracefully transition out of youth while maintaining their own dignity and passion.[49]

Dreaming of tortoises is supposed to indicate introversion, hiding one's vulnerable feelings.[50] Modern superstitions include wearing a tortoiseshell bracelet as a talisman against evil and using tortoise oil as a painkiller. A more bizarre method of relieving pain is to hang a tortoise foot on the good foot of a gout sufferer.[51] In the 1960s a two-foot-long tortoise at a European hospital in Kenya was credited with curing back pain. Patients sat on the back of 'The Doctor', and within seconds lumbago and other backaches vanished. For instance, the chief laboratory technologist (*sic*) at the hospital, an Englishman who had had to give up golf because of back trouble, was cured almost immediately and was able to play five rounds a week. Some said it was an ancient remedy of the Kikuyu tribe and others that it emanated from the Zulus of South Africa.[52]

Over in Western Nigeria during millennium year, a 30-year-old woman, Tawa Ahmed from Ondo, claimed to have made medical history when, after a five-year pregnancy, she gave birth to a 2lb 2oz tortoise. Locals are well known for believing in miracles.[53] As elsewhere in the world and throughout human history, you believe in what you want to. Myth can be more powerful than reality.

3 Ancient and Modern

In their long history, tortoises have acquired associations, giving their name to something or being the basis of a particular belief. Some associations have died out or been transformed, the underlying belief remaining but no longer involving tortoises. Other associations have survived from the ancient to the modern world. Sometimes the modern world has looked back for an association.

For example, the prehistoric animal gave its name among archaeologists to a prehistoric technique of making stone tools. The technique, known as prepared- or tortoise-core, was widely used in Africa, Asia and Europe. It was an advance on the laborious process of trimming a piece of stone into a tool by removing a series of flakes. With the new method, preliminary flaking of a block of stone was aimed at shaping the block so that the wanted flake eventually detached, ideally with a single blow. The flake could then be used immediately as an implement, typically a straight-edged hand axe or skinning knife. The technique demanded more forethought and a higher degree of skill in early tool manufacture among primitive people, including the low-browed Neanderthals, who were superseded by *Homo sapiens*.[1] Perhaps of some practical benefit was the ancient Chinese art of divination, *chan*, with a tortoise shell. The practice flourished particularly at the court of the Late Shang dynasty, about 1200–1045 BC. A Bronze Age civilization with defined social classes and a bureaucracy, Shang was the first historic Chinese dynasty, about 1523–1027 BC, and the oracle bone inscriptions represent the earliest corpus of writing in East Asia. About 4,500 different characters have been identified. Easily deciphered were primitive picture forms such as a circle with a dot in the centre for the sun, and a semicircle mounted on the bar of a cross, for a cow.

Secure within the dome and base of its shell, the tortoise was regarded as a mediator between heaven and earth. Hence it was reckoned to possess the powers of knowledge and prophecy. In important matters, whether personal or those of state, it gave a yes/no decision, which was at least better than indecision and hence inaction. 'A dried tortoise shell has no will, yet it can predict the future.' This could involve agriculture ('Auspicious. We will receive abundant harvest'), building a settlement, a possible disaster ('There will be calamities'), interpretation of a dream, a hunting expedition, mobilizing for a military campaign, a weather forecast, which ancestor caused the toothache. A consultation (*pu*) could give a fortunate (*chi*) or unfortunate (*hsiung*) prediction or resolve doubts (*chi'i*). In a society where superstition was prevalent, oracles interpreted by diviners were compared with the opinions of people such as princes and ministers. Predictions were verified, for instance in childbirth: 'It was not good. It was a girl.'

Divination involved cleaning and polishing a tortoise shell, heating it with red-hot metal bars and interpreting the resulting stress cracks. The diviner interpreted on the basis of shape, sound or speed with which cracks appeared. Obviously a tortoise had to be killed beforehand, and since there were thousands of diviners practising this pseudo-science

A diviner's tortoise shell. Only diviners could interpret patterns of cracks such as these.

over some two millennia into the early centuries of the Christian era the particular species was rendered extinct. Their shells survived in temples, and archaeologists have unearthed scores of thousands on the site of the remains of the Shang dynasty capital in Anyang County, Henan Province, once an area teeming with tortoises, a favourite local food.[2] The practice was apparently condemned by the sage Confucius (551–479 BC).

This *c.* 1100 BC Babylonian boundary-stone, 'establisher of the boundary for ever', records the sale of a piece of corn-land to a high official. Curses were laid on anyone removing or defacing the landmark. The carved reliefs include tortoises.

The *Analects* record: 'The Master said, "Zang Sunchen built a house for his tortoise, with pillars in the shape of mountains and rafters decorated with duckweed. Had he lost his mind?"'

Confucius was blaming Zang Sunchen for his lack of wisdom, since, in providing his tortoise with lavish accommodation, he was either yielding to earlier superstition about the predictive properties of its shell or usurping a royal privilege.[3] When tortoises became scarce, through excessive culling and environmental changes, people used bamboo strips for divination instead, a practice that continues today. Shaking fortune sticks in a temple can indicate where one's future lies. Divination by tortoise shell has been commemorated in Chinese postage stamps of 1996 and 1999, each featuring an inscribed plastron.

Following the example of the Lydians in western Asia Minor, seafaring and trading Aeginetans were the first Europeans to issue coins, a simple portable means of exchange in the Mediterranean world.

The Mediterranean world was a natural home of tortoises, a fact recognized in myths, literature and technology. In ancient Greece, terracotta models occur in graves as a long-lived accompaniment to the departed. The first coins to be issued in Greece proper, the silver 'tortoises' of the island of Aegina, struck probably by the mid-sixth century BC, gave a durability to this new form of exchange, an advance on lumps of metal, tools and cattle. Symbolically, the coins may have been related to the sea-tortoise sign of Astarte, the Phoenician goddess of traders. The tortoise was also the symbol of Aphrodite, patron goddess of Aegina.

Aesop, the teller of tales who lived about this time, had chosen the creature for at least three of his fables as a way of spinning a moral lesson. The fable of how the tortoise got its shell relates that Zeus was angry because the animal was the exception in not coming to his wedding feast, preferring to stay at home. The creature was therefore condemned to carry its home on its back.[4] The tale of the tortoise and the eagle has the moral that rivalry leads to a disregard of wise counsel. When the eagle told the tortoise that he could not teach it to fly, the tortoise became the more importunate. Exasperated, the eagle bore him aloft in its talons and dropped him from a great height.[5] There was an eagle that, having opened tortoises in this way, ate them.

A similar fable occurs in Indian folklore, collected in the *Kacchapa Jataka*, where a tortoise is borne through the air by two birds holding a stick that the tortoise has clamped in its mouth. It falls to its death when it opens its mouth to answer the taunts of the birds. In one version, the future Buddha, Bodhisattva, offers it as a telling example to an incurably talkative king. After seeing the fallen tortoise in two pieces in the courtyard of his palace and having had the parable spelt out, the king became a man of few words.[6] A Tibetan version has the boastful tortoise saying to children below that it was not the egrets who were clever but he, who had devised the flight plan to the Heavenly Lake.[7] The Roman proverb on the impossible was 'The tortoise flies', the equivalent of the English 'Pigs might fly'. There is also the story that Aeschylus was killed at Gela in Sicily in 456 BC when an eagle, mistaking the tragedian's bald head for a rock, dropped a tortoise on it. The story occurs in Pliny the Elder's *Natural History* (x. 3), Valerius Maximus' first-century farrago of sententious examples, *Factorum ac dictorum memorabilium libri*, and in François Rabelais' sixteenth-century *Gargantua and Pantagruel* (iv. 17), but today scholars regard the story as apocryphal.

During 'A Voyage to Brobdingnag', the country of the giants in Jonathan Swift's *Gulliver's Travels* (1726), the hero endured a similar menace:

I heard a noise over my head like the clapping of wings,

and then began to perceive the woeful condition I was in, that some eagle had got the ring of my box in his beak, with an intent to let it fall on a rock like a tortoise in a shell, and then pick out my body and devour it; for the sagacity and smell of the bird enabled him to discover his quarry at a great distance, though better concealed than I could be within a two-inch board.[8]

Fortunately, the eagle dropped the box into the sea, from which Gulliver was rescued.

The most well-known and enduring of Aesop's fables is the one about the tortoise and the hare, the race going to the steady plodder.[9] Jean de La Fontaine retold it in verse in 1668, and Marianne Moore translated it into English verse in 1954.[10] Arthur Rackham (1867–1939), who delighted in illustrating fairy tales, made it one of his subjects. La Fontaine also retold the Indian folk tale about the two birds as *The Tortoise and the Two Ducks*.[11] The tortoise and the hare is a simple simile that soon makes its point. Malthus, who argued in his *Essay on the Principle of Population* (1798) that poverty was inevitable because population increases geometrically while food supply grows arithmetically, summed it up neatly: 'It would appear to be setting the tortoise to catch the hare.' A character flaw in William Makepeace Thackeray's *Pendennis* (1848) needs only a two-sentence description: 'He had slept and the tortoise had won the race. He had marred at its outset what might have been a brilliant career.'[12] Ambrose Bierce (1842–1914), the American sardonic humorist, gave the story a late nineteenth-century twist in *Aesopus Emendatus*:

A Hare having ridiculed the slow movements of a Tortoise was challenged by the latter to run a race, a Fox

John Vernon Lord's illustration of the hare and tortoise race.

Since 1968 McCormick Tractors has made a graphic distinction between fast and slow on its gear-boxes.

to go to the goal and be the judge. They got off well together, the Hare at the top of her speed, the Tortoise, who had no other intention than making his antagonist exert herself going very slowly. After sauntering along for some time he discovered the Hare by the wayside, apparently asleep, and seeing a chance to win pushed on as fast as he could, arriving at the goal hours afterwards, suffering from extreme fatigue and claiming the victory. 'Not so,' said the Fox; 'the Hare was here long ago and went back to cheer you on your way.'

Anita Brookner makes the same point in her novel *Hotel du Lac* (1984):

What is the most potent myth of all? . . . The tortoise and the hare . . . the hare is always convinced of his own superiority; he simply does not recognize the tortoise as a worthy adversary. That is why the hare wins.[13]

Modern humorists delight in turning the tale on its head. Slow and steady wins the race does not necessarily apply in a fast-changing world.

Elizabeth Jenkins made clear the theme of her novel *The Tortoise and the Hare* (1954). An autobiographical novel in feeling rather than fact, it deals with three principal characters: Imogen, devoted to her professionally successful husband Evelyn, and Blanche, the older lumpen neighbour, who steals him from Imogen. The characters live in three dimensions and their story is elegantly told, part of its appeal being the enigma of which woman is the tortoise and which the hare.

Tom Stoppard, who often bases his plays on marginal characters, featured the vulnerable creatures a hare, a tortoise and a goldfish fatally caught in philosophical demonstrations in *Jumpers* (1972). In *Arcadia* (1993), Plautus the Tortoise, sleepy enough to serve as a paperweight, is seemingly an unimportant character, but he turns out to be the link between past and present, the two time periods of the play.

In the 1990s the poet Carol Ann Duffy produced a dramatic monologue for *Mrs Aesop*:

On one appalling evening stroll, we passed an old hare snoozing in a ditch – he stopped and made a note – and then, about a mile further on, a tortoise, somebody's pet, creeping, slow as marriage, up the road. *Slow but certain, Mrs Aesop, wins the race.* Asshole.

What race? What sour grapes? What silk purse, sow's ear, dog in a manger, what big fish? Some days I could barely keep awake as the story droned on towards the moral itself. *Action, Mrs A., speaks louder than words.*

Mr Aesop is better at telling moral fables than he is in bed.

Another ancient Greek race, between Achilles and the tortoise, has not stood the test of time. The philosopher Zeno of Elea, who flourished around 500 BC, proposed the paradox of a race between the fleet Achilles, hero of the Trojan War, and the plodding tortoise. Since Achilles was able to run ten times faster, he gave his opponent 100 metres start, but he could not win the race because the tortoise ran 10 metres while he was running the first 100 metres, reaching the point where the tortoise had started. While Achilles runs ten the tortoise runs one; while Achilles runs one the tortoise runs one-tenth; and so on *ad infinitum.* In short, in the philosopher's paradox the tortoise is always ahead of Achilles, who cannot catch him up.

Leo Tolstoy deals with the question in the opening of Part XI of *War and Peace* (1865–6):

For the human mind the absolute continuity of motion is inconceivable. The laws of motion of any kind only become comprehensible to man when he examines units of this motion, arbitrarily selected. But at the same time it is from this arbitrary division of continuous motion

Animal cruelty is nothing new. On this red-figure *chous* (jug), Western Greek 360–350 BC, a girl in an elaborately patterned tunic is teasing a dog by dangling a tortoise in front of it.

into discontinuous units that a great number of human errors proceeds.

We all know the so-called sophism of the ancients, proving that Achilles would never overtake the tortoise, though Achilles walked ten times as fast as the tortoise. As soon as Achilles passes over the space separating him from the tortoise, the tortoise advances one-tenth of that space: Achilles passes over that tenth, but the tortoise has advanced a hundredth, and so on to infinity. This problem seemed to the ancients insoluble. The irrationality of the conclusion (that Achilles will never overtake the

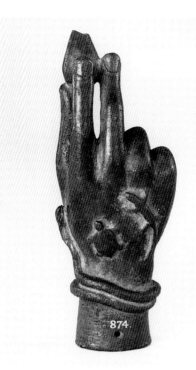

A Roman second- to third-century votive bronze hand of the Thraco-Phygrian god Sabazius. The hand, making a Latin blessing, bears cult symbols.

tortoise) arises from the arbitrary assumption of discon-nected units of motion, when the motion both of Achilles and the tortoise was continuous. By taking smaller and smaller units of motion we merely approach the solution of the problem.

Tolstoy goes on to examine the laws of historical motion, where precisely the same mistake arises.[14] There is a catch in the Achilles/tortoise conundrum; the solution is mathematical. For all their skill in geometry, what the Greeks lacked was a size lan-guage that could express the problem. Either algebraically

A graphic solution
to Zeno's paradox
of the Achilles
and tortoise race.

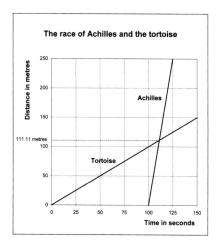

or by plotting distance against time, it can be shown that by running ten times faster Achilles could pass the tortoise after 111/9 seconds or 111.11 metres.[15]

A Greek mathematician of the Hellenistic period, Hero of Alexandria, who flourished in the first century AD, was also a practical inventor, notably of a bellows-operated organ and a steam engine that, although it demonstrated a principle, never went beyond a mechanical genius's toy. Among his inventions

Hero's labour-saving machine for moving heavy objects.

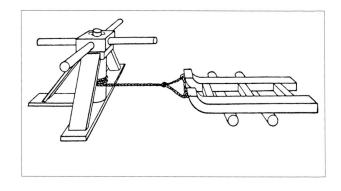

As Bacchus, the Roman god of wine, Pietro Barbino, court dwarf of Cosimo I, sits astride a tortoise on the 1560 fountain in the Boboli Gardens, Florence.

was a tortoise, a wooden frame or cradle resting on rollers. Dragged by the operation of a winch, it was a labour-saving way of moving heavy weights such as blocks of stone.

In Roman architecture *testudinatum* was a room with an arched roof. Inside, it might have complementary decoration. Before the Christian era, tortoiseshell, often obtained from turtles, was prized for its decorative value and traded. It was, for example, one of the exotic tropical products shipped from eastern Indonesia via the Philippines to southern China. During the first three centuries AD it found its way from India to the West, where the well-off in the Roman Empire used it for adornment. One of its applications was as a furniture veneer. Pliny comments in his *Natural History*: 'The practice of cutting tortoiseshell into plates and using it to decorate bedsteads and cabinets was introduced by Carvillius Pollio, a man of lavish talent and skill in producing the utensils of luxury.'[16] Carvilius Pollio flourished around 80 BC. In his *Ars Amatoria*, written around 1 BC, the erotic poet Ovid refers to hair clips of Cyllenian tortoiseshell, so-called from Mount Cyllene in Arcadia, where the god Mercury, the maker of the lyre, was born.

For the Romans, the tortoise, *testudo*, was a military formation. When attacking a walled town, the front row of soldiers would hold their shields in front of them while those behind held them above their heads. Seen from above by defenders, it looked like a tortoise. A Roman shield, *scutum*, was oblong, more than a metre long and less than a metre broad. It consisted of four layers: two of wood, one of canvas and one of leather. With an iron rim around top and bottom edges and a boss in the middle, it was an effective form of defence against arrows, spears, stones and torches. Ideally, missiles would roll off. Achieving maximum effect of the formation called for a disciplined approach to the enemy, a drill in which each rank advanced slightly more upright than the one behind. Protected by their shields, soldiers could get close up to a wall and make a breach in it. If the wall was not too high, other soldiers could clamber on the back of the tortoise and scale the wall. Should it be too high, then scaling ladders were used.

This piece of siegecraft was no match, however, for the sophisticated artillery designed by the Greek mathematician and inventor Archimedes against the Roman blockade of his home city Syracuse during the Second Punic War (218–202 BC). It was not until 212 BC, after two years of ineffectual blockade, that a night attack was possible under the familiar cover, during a festival when a weak place in the walls was betrayed to the besiegers. In the subsequent occupation of the city, Archimedes, absorbed in solving a mathematical problem, did not answer a question put to him by a hasty Roman soldier, who killed him.

Against Rome's more primitive enemies the technique was so effective that they copied it, as Julius Caesar notes in his account of the Gallic War (58–51 BC):

The Belgae have the same method of attacking a fortress as the rest of the Gauls. They begin by surrounding the whole circuit of the wall with a large number of men and showering stones at it from all sides; when they have cleared it of defenders, they lock their shields over their heads, advance close up, and undermine it.[17]

As Gibbon records, the technique was still being used in 626 AD when Constantinople was under siege: 'During ten successive days, the capital was assaulted by the Avars [allies of the Persians], who made some progress in the science of attack;

they advanced to sap or batter the wall, under the cover of the impenetrable tortoise.'[18] A development of the *testudo* was a movable siege-shed, a wheeled device that could carry armament such as a battering ram, which might be as heavy as an iron-shod beam to add weight to the assault. The technique did not end with the Roman Empire. Tortoise ships were ironclad warships used by the Korean navy to repel persistent invaders from southern Japan at the end of the sixteenth century. On land, siege engines remained in use until the seventeenth century. The engine also came to be known by another name now known to every English-speaking child through a nursery rhyme.

Looking into the origin of nursery rhymes for donnish relaxation as Regius Professor of Civil Law at Oxford, David Daube, an authority on Roman Law, came to the conclusion in 1956 that Humpty Dumpty was a *testudo* and published his findings anonymously. Daube's first clue was the bumpy rhythm of the nursery rhyme, suggesting that Humpty Dumpty was something more substantial than the usually depicted egg. In Daube's view, Humpty was a siege engine in the form of a giant tortoise with a penthouse. Specifically, it was used in the Royalist siege of Gloucester during the English Civil War (1642–51).[19] Gloucester, a Roundhead (Parliamentary) fortified city, stood in the way of a Royalist advance from Wales on London, held by the Parliamentary forces. So important was Gloucester that, on 10 August 1643, Charles I himself was with his forces outside the city, where the siege engine was to be used:

Humpty Dumpty sat on a wall.

The chronicler Rushworth reports that, at the suggestion of a Dr Chillingworth, the strategy was for the siege engine to be moved slowly forward on wheels, which would slide into the city ditch. In front of the engine was a bridge intended to rest on the defensive walls and provide access for the attacking infantry. This did not happen because the whole tortoise crashed down into the ditch:

Humpty Dumpty had a great fall.

Royalist cavalry rode in to try and rescue the situation, but they could do little:

All the King's horses and all the King's men
Couldn't put Humpty together again.

On 5 September 1643 Gloucester was relieved by the London apprentices in their trained bands.

That was just one battle the eponymous creature had lost by proxy. After all the ups and downs of its associations, the tortoise remained principally as a moral example. Meanwhile, on a wider scale over a much longer time it had many enemies, principally man, to contend with.

4 Exploitation

In spite of their apparently unpromising utility, tortoises were a human resource. They could not be harnessed for work but they were a source of food and medicine; their shells made durable ornaments or receptacles, even told fortunes; and the complete creature could be traded. Man has always exploited the creatures for his own purposes. Over almost ten centuries, for instance, Native American peoples took desert tortoises for practical and ritual use.

Powdered shell was believed to relieve upsets of the stomach and urinary tracts. Intact, the carapace was a natural container, and was used for bowls, ladles, children's spoons, scoops for digging or removing earth and pottery-making tools. Some of the vessels may well have been used in ceremonies, along with items such as necklaces and rattles, also made from shell. Rattles were made by securing the upper and lower shells together, inserting either small stones or hardened seeds, then sealing the openings, producing a kind of maraca. So highly valued were the instruments that they were traded. Other possible uses for bones were as divining pieces or game counters. Rock art and motifs in basketry suggest a symbolic significance. One group of Southern Paiute tempted young eagles with tortoise meat so that they could be raised to participate in ceremonies.

Tortoises were cooked and eaten, generally being roasted over a campfire in open landscape or in a community pit or boiled in stews. To ensure an adequate supply, tortoises were hunted, often with dogs, which picked up the scent of those ranging or located their burrows. They were either lured from burrows with water or dragged out with long hooks. Archaeological sites in the south-western USA where the desert tortoise was so used have been dated as early as 9,500 years ago and were in use until some 150 years ago. Thus in keeping with their view that land was a communal resource to be used during a lifetime and then handed on fit for the next generation, the native tribes did not exploit the tortoise to extinction. Not all tribes exploited tortoises and not all tribes for all purposes.[1]

Some countries held prohibitive superstitions about killing tortoises for food. For instance, the French voyager François

A 19th-century pendant rattle from Uganda.

Pyrard remarked after an early seventeenth-century visit to the Maldives in the Indian Ocean that the islanders 'never eat any kind of tortoise, saying that the animal has some kinship with man'.[2] The attitude of mariners was very different. They had no affinity with the land except as temporary visitors taking on board ship whatever they wanted without replenishing.

From the end of the fifteenth century, when European navigators began their voyages of discovery, the creatures were at the mercy of new groups of hungry and eager predators. Mariners became a new large-scale menace to populations that had thrived largely undisturbed for thousands of years. Sir Walter Raleigh (1552–1618), for example, who had sailed in search of El Dorado, noted in his *Discovery of Guiana* (1596): 'We found thousands of Tortugas eggs, which are very wholesome meate.' *Tortuga* was the Spanish version of the late Latin term *tortuca*. Daniel Defoe's Robinson Crusoe (the novel was published in 1719) was well provided for on his island:

> I had no need to be venturous, for I had no want of food, and of that which was very good too, especially these three sorts, viz. goats, pigeons and turtle, or tortoise, which added to my grapes, Leadenhall market could not have furnished a table better than I, in proportion to the company; and though my case was deplorable enough, yet I had great cause for thankfulness that I was not driven to any extremities for food, but had rather plenty, even to dainties . . .
>
> I was lord of the whole manor; or, if I pleased, I might call myself king or emperor over the whole country which I had possession of: there were no rivals; I had no competitor, none to dispute sovereignty or command

with me: I might have raised ship-loadings of corn, but I had no use for it; so I let as little grow as I thought enough for my occasion. I had tortoise or turtle enough, but now and then one was as much as I could put to any use.[3]

Tortoises were believed to have medicinal properties. In his essay *Of the Resemblance of Children to Fathers*, Montaigne (1533–1592) railed against inexpert and ignorant physicians, listing some of their quack remedies:

Even the choice of most of their drugs is in some way mysterious and divine: the left foot of a tortoise, the urine of a lizard, the dung of an elephant, the liver of a mole, blood drawn from under the right wing of a white pigeon; and for us colicky folk (so disdainfully do they take advantage of our misery) pulverized rat turds, and other such monkey tricks that have more the appearance of a magical enchantment than of solid science.[4]

The three witches round their cauldron in Shakespeare's play *Macbeth* (1606) would not have been familiar with tortoises, but in the opening of the final act of *Romeo and Juliet* (mid-1590s) Romeo goes to a poor apothecary for a powerful poison and 'in his needy shop a tortoise hung'. Leonard Mascall in his *Third Booke of Cattell* (1627) advised: 'If Sinews or Nerues bee broken or bruised . . . Yee shall lay thereon the flesh of a Tortue, . . . beaten with the powder of Mullenherbe.'

Particularly at risk were the giant tortoises of the western Indian Ocean and the eastern Pacific. A few years after 1691 when he had visited Rodrigues, a volcanic Indian Ocean island

350 miles east-north-east of Mauritius discovered by the Portuguese in 1645, Francis Legaut wrote a gourmet account of the giant tortoises:

> I have seen one that weighed 100 lbs and had flesh enough on it to feed a good number of men. This flesh is very wholesome and tastes something like mutton but 'tis more delicate. The fat is extremely white, and never congeals nor rises in your stomach, eat as much as you will of it. We all unanimously agreed 'twas better than the best butter in Europe. To anoint oneself with this oil is an excellent recipe for surfeits, cold, cramps, and several other distempers. The liver of this animal is extraordinary delicate, 'tis so delicious that one may say of it, it always carries its own sauce with it, dress it how you will.[5]

Tortoise broth was a delicacy. Legaut also reported: 'sometimes you may see two or three thousand of them in a flock, so that one may go above a hundred paces on their backs . . . without setting foot to the ground'. A little more than a century and a half later this was no longer so. The giant tortoises of Rodrigues had been eaten to extinction. 'A few crumbling fragments of land-tortoise shells, which fell to pieces on being picked up' were the only evidence of their existence found by a scientific expedition to the island in 1864.[6]

In the same part of the Indian Ocean, on the Mascarene Islands, there was a species of sprinting tortoise, large but possibly the world's only lightweight racing tortoise. Having no predators, the species evolved with thin shells and larger openings for their legs and head. Hence they were able to move faster than most other species. They could not outrun man, however, who arrived in the early 1600s and introduced predatory dogs.

Left to themselves, the tortoises had numbered thousands, moving around in large groups. The last of their line were killed in the early 1800s. Their past has been partly reconstructed from DNA taken from surviving bones found in caves on the Mascarene Islands, the bones being ground to fine powder, the DNA extracted and analysed by biochemists from the Natural History Museum in London.

In his record of the *Beagle*'s visit to the Galapagos Islands, Charles Darwin noted for 17 September 1835:

> After dinner a party went on shore to try to catch Tortoises, but were unsuccessful. These islands appear paradises for the whole family of Reptiles. Besides three kinds of Turtles, the Tortoise is so abundant that [a] single Ship's company have caught 500–800 in a short time.

From further observations his diary entry for 26–7 September mentioned:

> Some individuals grow to an immense size: Mr Lawson, an Englishman, who had at the time of our visit charge of the colony, told us that he had seen several so large, that it required six or eight men to lift them from the ground; and that some had afforded as much as two hundred pounds of meat . . . The flesh of this animal is largely employed, both fresh and salted; and a beautifully clear oil is prepared from the fat. When a tortoise is caught, the man makes a slit in the skin near its tail, so as to see inside its body, whether the fat under the dorsal plate is thick. If it is not, the animal is liberated; and it is said to recover soon from this strange operation.[7]

Darwin himself found it 'indifferent food'. To sailors, though, it was a luxury in the long weeks across the Pacific. Giant tortoises could be kept in holds as an alternative to salted meat.

A further menace to giant tortoises in their native environments was destruction of their habitats. The introduction of other animals such as pigs, which dig up nests, and goats led to competition for the available food. Young tortoises were also tasty meals, especially for rats. They added to the threat from birds of prey such as buzzards on Galapagos. When China leased Hong Kong to Britain in 1842, according to the *London Geographical Journal*, the only animals on the island were 'a few small deer, a sort of armadillo, and a land-tortoise'. With the advance of civilization they were to die out.

Shells were useful receptacles. Around 1570, eating and drinking from tortoiseshell vessels was recommended as a way of avoiding infectious disease. In his *African Hunting from Natal to the Zambesi* (1863), William Baldwin referred to 'a drink of muddy water . . . out of a dirty tortoise-shell'.

Tortoises were no longer as safe as they had been in myth. In the words of the Revd Sydney Smith:

> Every animal has its enemies. The land tortoise has two enemies – man and the boa constrictor. The natural defence of the land tortoise is to draw himself up in his shell, and to remain quiet. In this state, the tiger, however famished, can do nothing with him, for the shell is too strong for the stroke of his paw. Man, however, takes him home and roasts him – and the boa constrictor swallows him whole, shell and all, and consumes him slowly in his interior, as the Court of Chancery does a great estate.[8]

Mottled brown and yellow tortoiseshell, obtained from turtles, continued to be a fashionable material in ornamental objects for centuries. Objects such as armbands with incised ornament, pectoral ornaments, spoons, masks of human and animal forms were made in Melanesia and Micronesia and are now found in museums as examples of excellence in primitive art.[9] In their own environments, some objects could be accepted as currency for payment of a bride price.[10] Muslim workers in eleventh-century Cairo made tortoiseshell caskets, combs and knife handles. Medieval Christendom was not a great importer from infidels, though. Trade into Europe grew with imports from the New World.

Heated, tortoiseshell is one of the most plastic of raw materials and can be welded together without glue. When soft it can be twisted into all sorts of shapes, cut and carved. Moulded or inlaid into its final form, it can be given a high polish. In the seventeenth century the material was a favourite decorative veneer on baroque furniture. Inlays were combined with brass, pewter or copper. The 2nd Earl of Cork referred in his diary for 1632 to 'a cabbonett of Torties shell', and John Evelyn (1620–1706), the diarist, recorded in the entry concerning his visit to Dieppe on 21 March 1644:

This place exceedingly abounds in workemen that make and sell curiosities of Ivory and Tortoise shells, in which they turne, and make many rare toyes; and indeed whatever the East Indys afford of Cabinets, Purcelan, natural and exotic rarities are here to be had with aboundant choyce.

Boule furniture was named after André Charles Boule (1642–1732), a Parisian cabinetmaker to Louis XIV, who perfected but did not invent this distinctive marquetry technique. Carried on by Boule's sons, the technique enjoyed a long vogue and was imitated in the nineteenth century.

From the second half of the seventeenth century, smaller objects were fashionable: clock cases, picture and mirror frames, needle-cases, purses (sometimes with mother of pearl inlay), knife handles, snuff boxes, ornamental combs and toilet sets. Thus Alexander Pope (1688–1744) in his mock-heroic poem *The Rape of the Lock* (1712) observes in Belinda's Toilet: 'The Tortoise here and Elephant unite, / Transform'd to combs, the speckled, and the white.' With the French technique of *piqué*, gold and silver designs were laid on tortoiseshell that had been roughened by pricking holes in it. Persecution of Huguenot craftsmen in the later seventeenth century forced them to emigrate from France, taking the technique with them. It was adopted for items as diverse as chessboards, fans, lorgnettes, swordsticks and tea caddies.

Social and technical changes led to a reduced use of tortoiseshell as a material. From the early nineteenth century

The tortoise shell floor at St Katharine Docks, Port of London, c. 1930. London was the only open market in the world for this product, which would have been made up into items such as combs and spectacle frames. Weighed and graded, lots of shells were arranged in numbered bins ready for sale. The buyers wore bowler hats.

the taking of snuff declined and with it the need for so many snuff boxes. On the other hand the custom of leaving one's card grew and with it the demand for cardcases. Since the seventeenth century stained horn had been a cheaper substitute for the real thing. Stained celluloid was introduced about 1900. In the 1920s women who bobbed their hair needed fewer tortoiseshell combs. Modern plastics provided an inexpensive, turtle-friendly alternative to the natural material for articles such as combs and spectacle frames. Plastics are much more malleable and versatile than the thin shells of the genuine article and can be coloured to suit current fashion.

The supposed medicinal and food value of tortoise jelly and drinks lingered on, especially in Chinese society. Specific parts of turtle or tortoises, which the Chinese do not distinguish, their

A well-appointed tortoise jelly shop in Kowloon, Hong Kong. The last three characters refer to tortoise jelly.

Just inside the shop, tortoises gently heat over coals for conversion into jelly.

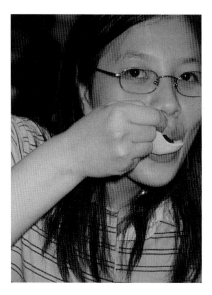

A young woman eats tortoise jelly to stay well.

Tortoise jelly is black.

eggs, blood or ground-up shell, are credited with wide-ranging applications: as aphrodisiacs, promoters of longevity, cures for dysentery, kidney problems, lethargy, lumbago and as an aid in difficult childbirths. Such is the demand in South-East Asia that many species are endangered. In November 1998, 250 tortoises were stolen from the Kek Lok Si temple in Malaysia. Concerned for their fate – a destination in cooking pots – the temple abbot pointed out that killing the creatures for food would contravene the tenets of Buddhism. In 1999 an illegal immigrant from China who broke into a Hong Kong home and ate a pet tortoise was jailed for a year. The normal sentence for burglary was three years, but the offender received a lesser penalty because he had shown no intent to steal, only to satisfy his hunger. T. S. Eliot (1888–1965) was responsible for the most bizarre satisfaction, in his obscene verses on 'The Jolly Tinker'. In scatological detail the verses recount the behaviour of the bawdy, lecherous seafarer Captain Colombo, who indiscriminately ravishes his male ship-mates, a cabin boy, a chaplain and even a tortoise.[11]

Where they occurred naturally, the creatures were readily available for the satisfaction of appetite during the Depression. Gopher tortoises extracted from their burrows, for example, were a major source of food for families in the south-eastern States of the USA. The popular American dish turtle pie, some-times known as terrapin tart, has nothing to do with the creatures: a rich dessert of chocolate, caramel, pecan nuts and almonds, it is not even shaped like a turtle.

In the West, though, it was as pets that tortoises were most exploited. At the end of the nineteenth century only a few hun-dred were imported each year. Knowledge of how to look after them was scarce. For instance, in the 'answers to correspon-dents' column in *The Girl's Own Paper* of 1 May 1880, the editor wrote: 'You do not state what kind of tortoises yours are. If the common, they may live in the garden, and eat vegetables.' Advice on 31 July was similarly curt: 'Ordinary tortoises some-times go to sleep for four months at a time. Put it in the garden, and it will select food for itself.'

During the early years of the twentieth century the imported numbers increased to thousands. In the 1930s they were sold for as little as sixpence (2½p) or a shilling (5p) outside schools and in markets along with goldfish and cheap, flimsy Japanese toys. A common US price was 35 cents. At these prices, the crea-tures were regarded as expendable. Like goldfish, they were given away as prizes at fairgrounds and any remaining in a crate or cardboard box when the fair moved on were often left to the mercy of ignorant schoolboys scavenging the site. There were music hall and seaside postcard jokes about hungry drunks coming out of pubs buying and trying to eat tortoises under the impression that they were crusty meat pies. Pet shop owners promoted them as cheap pets scavenging for grubs in the garden and eating old greenery scraps. A frequently heard comment from former owners was 'We had a tortoise but . . .'. Towards the end of the decade, concern for their fate was mounting. One objection was to tortoise racing on pub billiard tables, which was allegedly gaining popularity.[12]

Frederick Hobday, president of the Universities' Federation for Animal Welfare, took up the more serious issue of the tortoise traffic in a letter to *The Times* of 6 December 1938, pointing out that tens of thousands of North African tortoises were imported each year to be sold as pets. Most of their purchasers were quite unaware that the creatures are sun-loving herbivores, and had to be provided with a large quantity of suitable food, fresh drinking water and adequate shelter to survive. Only 1 or 2 per cent lived through their first winter. During their voyage they were crowded in layers in small, open crates, many of them packed on their backs to economize on space. Many suffered broken shells and crushed limbs during transport. They were also imported simply as ballast. It appeared that the tortoises remained in their crates (in one case the crates were known to be stacked in a cellar) until required for immediate sale, or were left in heaps in small yards or on roofs. The National Council of Women had already con-sented to take action, and Frederick Hobday hoped that many other bodies and individuals would use their influence to secure improvements in this objectionable traffic.

Captain Fergus MacCunn, chief secretary of the Royal Society for the Prevention of Cruelty to Animals (RSPCA), immediately followed up, adding that formerly tortoises were shipped packed in barrels and stowed under boilers. Mortality was high. The RSPCA made representations to shippers, who finally agreed to send the creatures in crates. It was

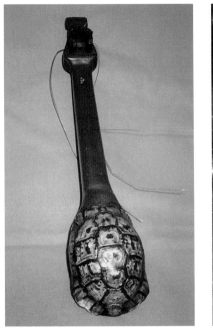

subsequently found that the crates were unsatisfactory and an RSPCA inspector suggested that the design should be altered for better ventilation and to avoid damage to the protruding limbs and heads of tortoises. In poor districts, where unscrupulous dealers sometimes sold tortoises 'to keep down black beetles', enquiries from pupils at school meetings revealed that many children owned tortoises but did not know how to look after them. Given proper care tortoises would live here for many years. Even so, the import of more than two million quoted to the RSPCA by a shipper in 1938 could not really be justified.[13] At a source of the trade, the Animal Welfare Society of South Africa was concerned about the extermination of highly ornamental

A 19th-century North African lute has a creative element so markedly absent from modern tourist 'souvenirs' in the same region.

Varnished 'souvenirs' in a Tunisian gift shop.

'geometric' tortoises to satisfy demand in Europe and America.[14]

Lieutenant-Colonel Leonard Noble of Henley-on-Thames, Oxfordshire, recounted his experience:

> I believe the usual way of disposing of these animals is by hawking them about in the mean streets of our larger towns at a price 'within the reach of us all'. I have two here, one was picked up off the main road to Reading, the other in a wood. Both had probably been turned adrift to fend for themselves, when the novelty of their possession had worn off.[15]

There were also instances of cruelty, typically by 10- and 12-year-old schoolboys breaking the shells by throwing the creatures or attacking them with bricks and other heavy objects. The RSPCA brought prosecutions, had the patched up victims produced as evidence and were successful in having the offenders placed on probation. Cruelty by children was nothing new. A girl painted on a Greek vase of the fourth century BC is shown dangling a tortoise by a string tied to one of its back legs. She is using it to tease a dog looking up from below.

An unusual form of cruelty was discovered in a box left by a woman passenger on a Paris–London flight of Imperial Airways in the spring of 1929. In the box was a live tortoise wrapped in pink cotton wool and the back of its shell was studded with rubies, emeralds and other coloured stones. Perhaps the passenger had taken the idea from Joris Karl Huysmans's novel of 1884, *A Rebours* (*Against Nature*). Dealing with the artificial, extravagant existence of the *fin-de-siècle* aristocrat des Esseintes, it was described by a British critic as the 'breviary of decadence'. A similar creature made its appearance in J. K. Rowling's novel *Harry Potter and the Prisoner of Azkaban* (1999), where there was 'a magical creature-shop' in which 'a gigantic tortoise with a jewel-encrusted shell was glittering by the window'.[16]

After the comparatively mild protests, the pet trade continued for almost another half century. In the mid-1970s Britain was still importing more than half a million tortoises a year from Morocco, a rate that worried the International Union for Conservation of Nature and Natural Resources. Although the Moroccan Government prohibited the export of tortoises below a certain size, many of the smaller creatures were killed and their top shells made into a type of banjo. Tourists lacking both ear and sense bought some 10,000 of these instruments a year.

The only real respect was for giant tortoises, usually in zoos. Their size, rarity, statistics of age and weight made them unusual within their class of reptile. People from the 2nd Lord Rothschild to young children were photographed sitting on them. Of all the tortoises they were the popular ones chosen to appear alongside great creatures like elephants, lions, tigers, rhinoceros and so on in animal series on cigarette cards. On the back of the card they were billed as the longest lived creature.

Because of their small size and their ability to survive on restricted diets, Soviet scientists chose tortoises over dogs as crew in the Zonds satellites that orbited the moon and they were brought back safely to earth in 1968 and 1969.

The plight of the exploited creature is well caught in H. E. Bates's short story *The Day of the Tortoise* (1961). Fred, 58, a lonely drudge looking after three eccentric older sisters, is likened to his pet tortoise, William, tethered by several yards of string tied (ouch!) to one of its legs. When William reached the limit of its string it halted, unable to escape. Indoors it scraped its feet to no purpose on the bare wood floor, 'an unhappy marching prisoner there on the treadmill'. Fred has a brief fling with the girl from the dairy, to the disapproval of his sisters, but

Tortoise 'banjos' in a Moroccan *souk*.

Bellows on sale in Morocco.

Egyptian tortoises, an endangered species, on sale in a Cairo market.

top right: Live tortoises are displayed in a plastic basket without food in a Tunisian market.

Charles Waterton (1782–1865), eccentric naturalist, created this tortoise carrying two bags, the crushing burden of the £800 million National Debt. On top of the tortoise is a warlike devil, perhaps a reference to the Napoleonic War that had raised the level of debt, and around it are the obsequious, mocking devils that may be the fundholders who profited from the interest paid on the debt.

it comes to nothing. Similarly, William the tortoise, once thought to have escaped, was hiding behind the compost heap.

The most bizarre exploitation occurred among the Galapagos Islands in 2000/2001, when in their dispute with conservationists over fishing quotas local fisherman took tortoises hostage, ransacked a research station and harassed tourists. Galapagos tortoises were giant bargaining counters in an increased quest for delicacies such as lobsters, sea cucumbers and shark fins.

There were many exploiters of the creatures, mainly for money. Fortunately, they were outnumbered by those who respected them for themselves. Unfortunately, the latter were not as powerful.

5 Appreciation

Tortoises were exploited in reality. They were also honoured in references harking back to the virtues enshrined in myths, in art and as lifelong companions by some careful owners.

Endurance of myth was most marked in China. Cao Cao (AD 155–220), poet and warlord of Wei in northern China, celebrated tortoise attributes:

> Fabled tortoise – long living
> Yet his span is set,
> Mighty basilisk – cloud soaring
> Must end in dust and ashes,
> Old steed in paddock grazing
> Yearning for long past races,
> Stout hero in his twilight years˙
> His resolution knows no ending,
> Success and failure, now up now down
> For each there comes a time,
> Nor does this rest alone with heaven
> So foster delight – nurture pleasure,
> And you may live forever.[1]

Cao Cao has been compared to a later warlord and poet who also wrote about the tortoise, Chairman Mao. Tortoise

attributes were acknowledged in two medieval contributions to Chinese knowledge. Under the Sung dynasty (960–1279), juristic writings recording decisions in causes célèbres were compiled into the Tortoise Mirror of Case Decisions (*Che Yu Kuei Chien*). Accumulated wisdom was thus preserved for reference.[2] A mid-fifteenth-century treatise on laboratory preparations for producing a heart elixir harked back to a traditional Chinese belief about the design of a furnace. It recommended using a tortoise-shaped combustion chamber, the top being the pattern of the sky and the bottom representing the earth.[3] Although less effective than a chemical elixir, imitating the movements of long-lived tortoises and cranes was supposed to produce good results for health and hearing. Teacher Ning's 'tortoise' breathing exercise involved the subject grasping and hanging from a rope in various ways.[4]

In the Temple of Literature, Hanoi, stout tortoises support stelae recording scholars' achievements.

Within the Chinese Empire, the way into the senior ranks of the governing class was by examination, mainly in the tenets of the sage Confucius. Officials were trained and selected, for example at the Temple of Literature built in Hanoi in 1070. Dedicated to Confucius, it was also the site of the first university (1076) established in that part of the Empire. In 1484 Emperor Le Thanh Tong ordered that stelae recording the names and academic achievements of the laureates who had passed the triennial examinations should be erected there, starting in 1442. Altogether 112 stelae were erected, of which 82 survive with the names of 1,306 successful scholars. Each stele is carried on the back of a tortoise as a symbol of strength and longevity – appropriate, since the exams were not easy to pass. In 1733, out of some 3,000 entrants, only eight passed the 35-day doctoral examination and became mandarins. Stone tortoises as stele bearers were first used in the sixth century AD but were reserved for the three highest grades of officials and the imperial family.

One symbol of longevity was the large sculpture tortoises in Karakorum, the early capital of the Mongol Empire. After making many conquests, Genghis Khan (1162–1227), 'Very Mighty Ruler', established his headquarters at Karakorum in 1220. In 1235 his son and successor Ögödei decided to make it a more distinguished capital of the enlarged empire by building walls, a palace and other permanent places. Empires rise and fall. In 1267 Kublai Khan (1216–1294) moved the capital to what is now Beijing, the capital of China, and Karakorum declined. It was partly rebuilt after 1368, when the last emperor of the Mongol dynasty of China was banished from Beijing and returned to the original capital. This was later destroyed, partly rebuilt and then abandoned. A local story was told that the head of a monastery had one of the stone tortoises placed on the way to a nunnery, reminding monks of their vows when making their nocturnal

exploits. Today these tortoises, one on the site of the ancient capital, remain as a tourist attraction, the oldest substantial reminder of what was once the heart of a great empire. Fitzroy Maclean recounted his experience in *To the Back of Beyond* (1974):

A surviving remnant of the once great Mongol Empire, the stone tortoise at Karakorum bears prayer flags in the Tibetan Buddhist tradition.

> Not much more than a century after Genghis's conquest of China, the Chinese . . . drove back the Mongols, and, turning the tables on them, utterly destroyed their capital of Karakorum. Today, as we found when we finally arrived there, nothing of its former magnificence remains but a solitary stone tortoise, derelict and disconsolate, on which every now and then a passer-by drops a pebble or two, out of a vague deference to its presumed holiness. Having added ours to the pile we went on our way. [5]

Some 48 km northwest of Beijing on the concourse for the funeral processions of the emperors being buried in the Ming tombs a tortoise bears the largest stele in China. Made in 1425, the stele records the names of the Ming emperors buried in the necropolis.

Beyond the entrance to the tombs of the Ming dynasty (1368–1644) is the double-roofed, four-doored stele pavilion, which contains the largest stele in China, standing on a stone tortoise. The stele bears the names of the thirteen Ming emperors buried in the valley, some 48 kilometres north of Beijing.

Inspired by a visit to China in 1983, a German artist, Joachim Schmettau, produced for a square in Berlin-Charlottenburg a sculpture of a young man astride a tortoise with the inscription: 'Alles verzehrt am ende / Die eine macht / Die macht / Der zeit'. A German version of an anonymous Japanese haiku of unknown date, it can be translated as: 'Everything will be consumed. There is one power and that power is time.' Man spends his short life in slow-moving time.

The tortoise in its supporting role was formerly thought to have been used by the Italian goldsmith Benvenuto Cellini

114

(1500–1571) in the gold and enamel Rospigliosi Cup (New York, Metropolitan Museum of Art), a scallop-shaped bowl mounted on the back of a tortoise. This has now been identified as a nineteenth-century forgery. Perhaps the forger took his inspiration from a design in bronze by Cellini's rival Leone Leoni (1509–1590) for a salt container. At the beginning of the seventeenth century Queen Elizabeth I of England was presented with 454 'buttons of gold like tortoises, in each one a pearl' as a New Year gift. Gilt bronze was the material for a seventeenth-century south German clockwork model of a tortoise (turtle?) with a trident-waving merman riding on its back (Victoria & Albert Museum, London). When the mechanism is wound, the trident waves and the tortoise moves.

Joachim Schmettau's sculpture in Berlin-Charlottenburg was inspired by a Japanese *haiku* on man's brief existence in the aeons of the universe.

Kyoto, until 1868 the capital of Japan, is also the nation's chief Buddhist centre. In the Toji temple a tortoise supports a stele.

During the seventeenth century, when plate armour had been abandoned in favour of increased mobility, improvements in firearms forced armourers to increase the thickness and weight of their products. More powerful bullets led to thicker armour to resist them. So weighty iron shields were produced in the form of a tortoise's shell.

One of the arts of peace was the association of the creature with pottery from the mid-seventeenth century. At Arita in Japan, the first Kakiemon, a porcelain maker, is reputed to have learned the technique of colour enamelling around 1644, three years after the Dutch were given a trading concession. Soon large quantities of Arita ware were being shipped to the Netherlands. One of the forms of decoration was a water-tortoise trailing waterweed. While the Japanese called it the 'raincoat tortoise', because the trailing weed resembled their straw raincoat, through a misunderstanding it was known in

Using as his major source Matteo Ricci's *Commentaries* (1615), the account of fellow Jesuit missions in China, 1582–1610, Athanasius Kircher (1601–1680) produced his illustrated *China Monumentis* (1667), a description of Chinese civilization.

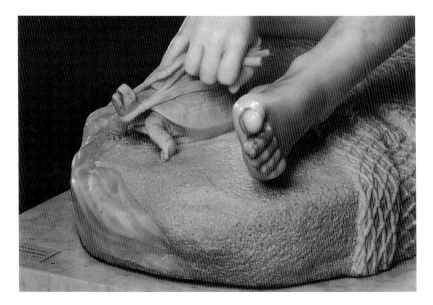

François Rude's marble sculpture of a Neapolitan fisher boy playing with a tortoise (1831–3), now in the Louvre, Paris, earned him the Légion d'Honneur and a commission to work on the Arc de Triomphe.

Europe as 'flaming tortoise'. This became the name of the design when it was adopted in Chelsea porcelain in the eighteenth century.[6] 'Tortoiseshell ware' is the name given to mid-eighteenth-century Staffordshire earthenware that has a mottled, usually brown, lead glaze. Thomas Whieldon (1719–1795) is the name most associated with the process, which used manganese brown, copper green and cobalt blue for the translucent glazes.[7]

The shape of the tortoise lends itself to sculpture, large or small. An amusing neo-Classical marble piece by François Rude (1784–1855) of a young nude Neapolitan fisher boy playing with a tortoise, holding it back with a reed, can be seen in the Louvre. The piece (1831–3) earned Rude the cross of the Légion d'honneur and he went on to execute in 1836 his best-known work, the heroic relief *Le Départ* (of the volunteers of 1792, who

Another example of Edward Lear's illustrations from J. E. Gray's *Tortoises, Terrapins and Turtles Drawn from Life* (1872). This is of the common spider tortoise with its distinctive markings.

left to fight the Austrians and Prussians invading from the Netherlands) on the east façade of the Arc de Triomphe in Paris. Another nineteenth-century French sculptor, Henri Jacquemart (1824–1896), captured in bronze a dog looking at a tortoise. In the twentieth and twenty-first centuries Venetian glass makers have modelled the animals.

In 1879 in the USA, Charles Portway of Halstead, Essex, patented the Tortoise Slow Combustion Stove. Made in the Tortoise Foundry at Halstead, the stoves were used mainly in barracks, churches, meeting halls and schoolrooms; special models were made for boilers, greenhouses, harness rooms, laundries, portable use, ships and trades such as plumbers and tinsmiths. The 'Cheerful' model had an ornamental door with mica panels. In the First World War the Tortoisette was developed for burning anthracite, and in the 1960s the Tortoisaire oil-fired heating system was produced. Alas, the old-world appeal of the Tortoise Ornamental Stove, with sales of

Panzer Leader lived in the garden of Scottish poet Ian Hamilton Finlay. Tortoises have been described as Tanks with Attitude.

Many an army barrack room was heated by a Tortoise stove.

The Newest Slow Combustion Close Stove,

THE "CHEERFUL" TORTOISE.

DESCRIPTION.

This Stove is a combination of the sterling qualities of the well-known "Tortoise" Slow Combustion Stove, with the advantage of that comfortable feeling derived from a fire that can be seen.

The front of the Stove is fitted with a strong ornamental door, with mica panels through which a bright and mellow glow is diffused. The fire is kept from actual contact with the door by the front bars; and cinders, dropping through the openings in the bars fall into the ash receptacle at the bottom. The front and bottom grates can be easily removed with poker for cleaning out or renewal.

A loose and movable grate is fitted to the bottom of the Stove, and any ashes accumulating on the grate can be removed by pushing the short lever on side of Stove backwards and forwards once or twice. The draught is arranged on the well-known "Tortoise" principle, and can be set to keep the Stove burning from 12 to 24 hours without attention.

Ordinary gas coke broken small is the best and cheapest fuel, but anthracite coal will burn longer without attention.

Horizontal Nozzles sent unless otherwise ordered.

With Horizontal or Vertical Smoke Nozzle.

(5)

The approximate time the Stove will burn without attention is as follows:

	With Coke.		With Anthracite Coal.
No. 1—	7 to 9 hours.	...	9 to 11 hours.
„ 2—10 to 12	„	...	12 to 14 „
„ 3—12 to 14	„	...	15 to 20 „
„ 4—14 to 18	„	...	20 to 25 „

	Total Height.	Diameter of Cylinder.	Diameter of Bottom.	Outside Diameter of Smoke Nozzle.	Heating Capacity.	
No. 1 ...	22 in.	... 8½in.	... 13in.	... 3¼in.	... 2,000 cubic feet	... No. 1
„ 2 ...	29¾in.	... 10in.	... 14in.	... 3¾in.	... 6,000 „	... „ 2
„ 3 ...	31½in.	... 12in.	... 16in.	... 4¼in.	... 10,000 „	... „ 3
„ 4 ...	38 in.	... 14in.	... 18in.	... 4¾in.	... 15,000 „	... „ 4

	PRICES £ s. d.		Ashes Pans. s. d.
No. 1 ...	3 10 0	...	3 0
„ 2 ...	4 10 0	...	4 0
„ 3 ...	6 0 0	...	6 0
„ 4 ...	8 0 0	...	8 0

TRAYS
For use on wood or carpet floors.

No. 1	2	3	4
11/-	13/-	18/-	25/-

10,000 a year in its heyday and noted by John Betjeman in his poem *Christmas* (1954) has been overtaken by modern central heating appliances. Today an example is most likely to be found in a redundant church.

Soon after the Tortoise Stove came into use, the 'tortoise' tent made its appearance. This was the popular name given to the enclosure used in hospitals to help patients with respiratory problems breathe more easily by containing an atmosphere richer in oxygen. Thus the *Daily News* reported on 8 April 1890: 'The patients found every care bestowed upon them in the tortoise tent.' It was a simple piece of equipment much needed when lung function was seriously impaired in pea soups, the thick yellow city smogs. Upper-class hospitals such as the Portland in London could pride themselves on offering the facility. Shape gave way to content and, in the twentieth century, the term oxygen tent became common.

A less flattering comparison of shape was made by the naturalist W. H. Hudson (1841–1922) when seeking summer lodging:

> Going on to the open front door I knocked, and after a time my summons was answered by the landlady, a person of a type to be met with occasionally not in Sussex only but all over the country, the very sight of which causes the heart to sink; a large, heavy-bodied, slow-minded and slow-moving middle-aged woman, without a gleam of intelligence or sympathy in her big expressionless face, a sort of rough-hewn preadamite lump of humanity, or gigantic land-tortoise in petticoats.[8]

After studying music in Munich and Leipzig, Otto Jägermeier (1870–1933), a friend of Richard Strauss, produced progressive symphonic works such as *Psychoses*, *In the Depth of the Sea*, *Battle of the Titans* and *The Physiological Feeble Mindedness of Woman*. Unaccountably, in 1907 he emigrated to the French colony of Madagascar. From then on he was considered dead in Europe; he could never get a publisher for his compositions; he sought no contact whatsoever with his European friends and acquaintances; and his musical work fell into oblivion. Rumour spread that he no longer existed. In Madagascar he kept as a pet a giant tortoise, which he used to take for walks on a lead. Perhaps an indication of his state of mind is the name that he gave to his pet, Rosi, after Don Quixote's horse Rosinante. Jägermeier's return to Europe in 1933 shortly before his death did not rescue his reputation immediately. Like his favourite creature, it took time. Fittingly, when the Musikinstitut Otto Jägermeier was founded in Berlin in his honour, a tortoise was adopted as its symbol. Gradually his work is being recognized with occasional public performances. Otto Jägermeier was not unique in taking a tortoise on his walks. Another was his contemporary, the wealthy French poet and eccentric bisexual Comte Robert de Montesquiou-Fezensac (1855–1921), who is believed to be the model for Proust's character Baron Charlus.

Mythical attributes of the tortoise were called upon in the USA in three wars, in 'hot' wars pejoratively and in the Cold War enthusiastically. On the Union side in the Civil War (1861–5), the man dubbed the Great American Tortoise was General George B. McClellan, at the outbreak of the war regarded as the most redoubtable opponent of the Southern armies. Cautious in his approach, though, he was twice defeated by the smaller armies of Robert E. Lee and, even when he had a greatly superior force at Antietam Creek, he could only draw, and failed to pursue Lee. President Lincoln said that McClellan was a general afflicted with 'the slows', and in the second year of the war relieved him of his command.

In the Second World War, another American president, Franklin D. Roosevelt, used the creature as a metaphor in a radio Fireside Chat of 23 February 1942 designed to fight defeatism:

Those Americans who believed that we could live under the illusion of isolationism wanted the American eagle to imitate the tactics of the ostrich. Now, many of these same people, afraid that we may be sticking our necks out, want our national bird to be turned into a turtle . . . I know I speak for the mass of the American people when I say that we reject the turtle policy.

In the Cold War, when Americans feared a Soviet atomic attack, the US Government created a subsidiary of the Department of Defense, the Office of Civil Defense. An element in its survival instructions during the 1950s was a black and white cartoon character, Bert the Turtle. A short film showed what to do when an atomic bomb hit and there was a bright flash:

Deedle Dum Dum
Deedle Dum Dum
There was a turtle by the name of Bert
And Bert the Turtle was very alert
When danger frightened him he never got hurt
He knew just what to do
He'd duck and cover
Duck and cover
He did what we all should learn to do
You and you and you and you
Duck and cover!
Remember what to do friends
Now shout it right out loud

What do you do when you see the flash?
DUCK AND COVER!

That was the way to avoid the effects of nuclear Armageddon.
The European explorations led to people keeping tortoises
as novel pets. From 1633 Archbishop Laud kept one at Lambeth
Palace, the London home of the archbishops of Canterbury. It
survived a horse ferry capsize in the River Thames and his master's beheading in 1645, but it was unfortunately killed while in
hibernation in 1753 by a gardener with a spade. The shell
complete with the lateral incision from the spade is preserved at
Lambeth Palace.

Keeping one of these ancient creatures was a lesser version of
the eighteenth-century hobby of keeping a hermit. Seeing a
tortoise stare in front for what seemed hours, contemplating a
leaf, one is reminded of William Blake's *Songs of Innocence* (1789):

To see a World in a grain of sand,
And a Heaven in a wild flower,
Hold infinity in the palm of your hand,
And Eternity in an hour.

Such was the attention that Gilbert White devoted to
Timothy, 'the old Sussex tortoise' who came from Ringmer. In
1923 the American ambassador unveiled the village sign, in
which Timothy has centre prominence over two Anglo-
Americans who married local girls: John Harvard, who gave his
name to the university, and William Penn, the Quaker founder
of Pennsylvania. On 1 January 2000, to mark the new millennium, John Fletcher, the chairman of Ringmer parish council,
officially inaugurated a new clock. Atop the brick structure, 5.2
metres high and paid for by public subscription, was a wrought-

Gilbert White's Timothy, 'the old Sussex tortoise', is prominent on Ringmer village sign.

Timothy atop Ringmer's millennium clock.

iron weathervane of Timothy Tortoise, the enduring symbol of Ringmer, a quiet village where time goes slowly.

Lord Rothschild, an accomplished naturalist, was particularly fond of large tortoises, which he kept at his country home, Tring in Hertfordshire. He enjoyed being photographed astride them. At Penshurst Place in Kent, Viscount de L'Isle has had some 60 small specimens on what is known as tortoise terrace.

Oriel College, Oxford, adopted its original tortoise as a mascot in about 1896, the creature becoming so familiar that it was elected an honorary vice-president of a College society. An undergraduate found a companion for it in his bed. When the mascot died in 1923 it was stuffed. So lifelike was the result that one of the fellows, finding it in the common room, took it out into the sun. The living tradition continued with two tortoises on whose shells were blazoned the College arms. On 28 May

1938 a tiny tortoise appeared in a quadrangle by the side of the other two, with *Ichabod* inscribed across its shell. His birth was announced on 31 May in *The Times*: 'TESTUDO, to Georgina, wife of O. C. Testudo, a son (Whalley George).' He was believed to be the only tortoise to have his birth announced in *The Times*. George Whalley was the honorary secretary of Oriel College Boat Club, which had the tortoise as its emblem and which in Eights Week had failed to come head of the river. On the first night that the college boat made a bump (touching the boat in front of it), Georgina laid an egg. The next day, when the boat made another bump, a second egg was laid, but there were no more bumps or eggs, provoking the provost's observation that we will never know whether Georgina's productivity would have continued in arithmetic or geometric progression. Only the provost's wife or daughter could properly give birth within the College precincts, and sometime after the appearance of the birth notice in *The Times* an academic colleague of the provost said that he was unaware that the provost's daughter had married an Italian. Testudo II was much kidnapped by under-graduates from other colleges. To his displeasure, other tortoises, some having the names of fellows painted on their backs, were added to the College collection. When he died in 1949 the provost penned a short elegy:

All his slow life he kept his secret well
Of what he loved and hated and believed;
It died with him, and we whom he deceived
Interrogate in vain his empty shell.[9]

His successor, Old L, had an L for Learner plate. One day he did get out and made his way into the High, where he was run over by a Post Office van. Old L was returned unharmed, but the

Post Office claimed the cost of repairing the van's suspension. Out of sympathy for his bachelor existence, some members of the College bought him four wives, but he killed them in an excess of sexual ardour by turning them over on their backs.

In another Oxford college, Corpus Christi, the tortoise was naturally known as the Corpoise Tortoise. Gonville and Caius College, Cambridge, had tortoises with the College crest painted crudely on their backs in Tree Court. They tugged at the porters' trouser cuffs to be fed. Unfortunately, they could wander out of the Gate of Humility into busy Trinity Street.

Timothy became a popular name for pets. Tommy is common, but the most well known is the one who, in 1997, was emotionally buried by his owner for some 20 hours after being lifted apparently dead from the fish pond. He rose from the dead, having shut down his metabolism and survived with practically no oxygen. Shelly occurs as a pun on the poet's name, Bysshe as his middle name. Pedro is apt for a sizeable Brazilian. Railways were the source for two contrasting specimens: Rocket, the mover, and Aslef (Associated Society of Locomotive Engineers and Firemen), who went slow, as did members of that trade union in the 1960s. Achilles, who enjoyed grapes and wild strawberries, was the name that Gerald Durrell gave to the sprightliest specimen he bought when growing up on the Greek island of Corfu, where he also watched tortoises erupting in unison from hibernation in the earth.[10] Also classically named was Madame Cyclops, who had one eye.

In 1960 the Oxford Union Society called a racing tortoise it had bought Gladstone, 'after our most illustrious president'. Oxford was the only British university to send the necessary dollar for the purchase of the tortoise and its entrance fee in the first international inter-university turtle race at Detroit University, Michigan, where he won seventh place. Travelling in a straw-lined cardboard box, Gladstone visited Germany, Austria, Switzerland, France, Italy, the Netherlands, Belgium and Ireland before arriving in Oxford. In every hotel he stayed at he had room service of lettuce and carrot.[11]

Justin Gerlach in his book *Famous Tortoises* (1998) lists Harriet, the name given in Australia to one of the Galapagos tortoises brought back by Charles Darwin, and Lonesome George, a survivor of the Pinta species, who is cared for at the Darwin Station on Santa Cruz island while the search continues for a mate. George, whose mate was killed in the early 1970s, is in danger of being the last of his line. In tortoise middle age, somewhere between 70 and 100 years old, until the end of the century George showed no interest in likely mates. Hope for the new millennium was expressed when DNA samples were taken from sub-species within the Galapagos Islands. The process involved rolling giant tortoises on their backs and extracting blood samples. DNA comparisons showed that George's close relatives were smaller creatures living 190 miles away on the other side of the archipelago.

Another Galapagos survivor, a single old male from Pinzon, 'began exhibiting amorous intentions with tortoise-shaped rocks' and was named Onan after the self-abuser in Genesis. Rotumah, a chief from a Pacific island, gave his name to a Galapagos tortoise later bought and ridden by Lord Rothschild. It suffered a different fate, dying of 'sexual over-excitation' 97 years after leaving his native habitat. He was a lusty old thing. Darwin, a giant tortoise at Blackpool Zoo, went through the motions every year with a female from Aldabra, but without result. When eight giant tortoises of a species thought to be extinct since the mid-nineteenth century were discovered on the Seychelles in 1997, the reason became obvious. Darwin was also a Seychelles survivor and could not cross-breed with an Aldabran.

Beatrice, Clio the muse of history, Esmeralda, Eve (naturally there is an Adam), Freda, Frederika, Gertrude, Josephine, Myrtle, Tara, Tilly, Thisbe and Titania from *A Midsummer Night's Dream* occur as female names. Myrtle the Turtle was the pet that survived Deforest Kelly, the actor who played Dr 'Bones' McCoy in the television series *Star Trek*. Most tortoises are regarded as 'he'. Male names include Adrian, Augustus, Barry, Beethoven, Boris, Brutus, Cerf (a Seychelles island), Chiron after the wisest and kindliest of the half human/half horse mythical centaurs, David and naturally his larger foe Goliath, Doddy, Gordon, Harold, Hector, Houdini, Humphrey, Jeremy, Jimmy, Joe(y), Lysander, Marmaduke, Max, Moses, Nicky, Phoenix, Quasimodo for his hunchback, Sammy, Sandy and Stan. Turbo was the name given to one that had a habit of running away and who managed to survive busy main roads.

Since it is not easy to determine whether a tortoise is male or female, unisex names are sometimes used: Go, Old Horrid, Shifty, Speedy, Surefoot, Swifty, Tiptoe and Tortee. Needle, one of a pair, had as a companion Fred. Ali Pasha was picked up by Henry Friston, a 21-year-old able seaman and one of nature's hoarders, under ten days' continuous fire on a crowded beach during the Gallipoli campaign of 1915. For a year Ali Pasha lived in a gun-pit on tomatoes as an unofficial mascot of the battleship HMS *Implacable*. The only Turkish prisoner of war still in British hands, he was brought back to England, where he was cared for by members of the Friston family. In 1968 he was made an honorary life member of the Tail-Waggers' Club, the 70,000 strong Australian dog welfare organization, because 'he hails from Gallipoli and the fact that a soldier amidst all the horror of War thought to care for a creature so unlikely as a Tortoise'. His fame spread round the world. When he died, of runny nose syndrome and kidney failure, in Suffolk in 1987 he was probably over 100 years old. He left no issue.[12]

References in literature draw on tortoise attributes. The prolific French novelist Honoré de Balzac (1799–1850) was fond of tortoise similes, for example regarding a detachment of soldiers marching up a mountain as 'creeping like an elongated tortoise', an invulnerable woman as a tortoise in her shell, or one retreating from an attic window like a tortoise drawing in its head, or another moving with the slowness of a tortoise. A fat wife in *Les Paysans*, the final and posthumously published novel in his panoramic series *La Comédie humaine*, is quickly characterized:

> No efforts could retain her waist-belt in its natural place. Bebelle candidly admitted that prudence forbade her wearing corsets. The imagination of a poet or, better still, that of an inventor, could not have found on Bebelle's back the slightest trace of that seductive sinuosity which the vertebrae of all women who are women usually produce. Bebelle, round as a tortoise, belonged to the genus of invertebrate females.[13]

Why should Balzac, an urban writer, use exotic similes so frequently? The explanation probably lies in his admiration for the zoological achievements of the French naturalist Jean Baptiste de Lamarck (1744–1829), who believed erroneously that the basis of evolution was the inheritance of acquired characteristics.

Early in *Crime and Punishment* (1866), Fyodor Dostoevsky describes the predicament of young self-absorbed Raskolnikov, who had led so cloistered a life that he was afraid of meeting anybody:

It would have been difficult to sink lower or be more untidy, but in his present state of mind Raskolnikov found it even pleasant. He had withdrawn from the world completely, like a tortoise into its shell, and even the face of the maid, whose duty it was to look after him and who sometimes came into his room, exasperated him beyond endurance.[14]

More fundamental was the creative approach to the structure of a story, akin to establishing the simplified prehistoric manufacture of a stone tool. Anton Chekhov (1860–1904), who emphasized character, mood and internal drama at the expense of plot, drafted his stories in full and then deleted the beginning and the end to leave the essence for his readers. This led John Galsworthy, best known for his *Forsyte Saga* (1906–22), tracing three generations of a family, to observe that Chekhov's stories were 'all middle, like a tortoise'.

The tortoise itself, a long-established creature, has earned itself places in world literature, occurring in prose, poetry and plays. With its many attributes, it has been a fertile source for writers, who each reflect their own distinctive personality from it.

English references tend to the kindly, for instance Lewis Carroll in *Alice in Wonderland* (1865): 'We called him Tortoise because he taught us.' A railway official explaining carriage charges for animals in the humorous weekly *Punch* (1869): 'Cats is "dogs" and rabbits is "dogs" and so's Parrats, but this 'ere "Tortis" is a insect, and there ain't no charge for it.' Edward Lear, writer of nonsense verse, worked with James de Carle Sowerby on illustrating Thomas Bell's *Tortoises, Terrapins and Turtles* (1872). Lear became fond of a tortoise, which he called T.

In his *Devil's Dictionary* (1906), the American sardonic humourist Ambrose Bierce (1842–1914) gave his definition: a creature thoughtfully created to supply occasion for the following lines by the illustrious Ambat Delaso:

To My Pet Tortoise

My friend, you are not graceful – not at all;
Your gait's between a stagger and a sprawl.

Nor are you beautiful: your head's a snake's
To look at, and I do not doubt it aches.

As to your feet, they'd make an angel weep.
'Tis true you take them in whene'er you sleep.

No, you're not pretty, but you have, I own,
A certain firmness – mostly your backbone.

Firmness and strength (you have a giant's thews)
Are virtues that the great know how to use –

I wish that they did not; yet, on the whole,
You lack – excuse my mentioning it – Soul.

So, to be candid, unreserved and true,
I'd rather you were I than I were you.

Perhaps, however, in a time to be,
When Man's extinct, a better world may see

Your progeny in power and control,
Due to the genesis and growth of Soul.

So I salute you as a reptile grand
Predestined to regenerate the land.

Father of Possibilities, O deign
To accept the homage of a dying reign!

In the far region of the unforeknown
I dream a tortoise upon every throne.

I see an Emperor his head withdraw
Into his carapace for fear of Law;

A King who carries something else than fat,
Howe'er acceptably he carries that;

A President not strenuously bent
On punishment of audible dissent –

Who never shot (it were a vain attack)
An armed or unarmed tortoise in the back;

Subjects and citizens that feel no need
To make the March of Mind a wild stampede;

All progress slow, contemplative, sedate,
And 'Take your time' the word, in Church and State.

O Tortoise, 'tis a happy, happy dream,
My glorious testudinous régime!

I wish to Eden you'd brought this about
By slouching in and chasing Adam out.

D. H. Lawrence (1885–1930) began his poem *Tortoise Family Connections*:

On he goes, the little one,
Bud of the universe,

Pediment of life.

and concluded *Baby Tortoise*:

All life carried on your shoulder,
Invincible fore-runner.

Ogden Nash (1902–1971), the American humorous poet, made a neat comment on *The Turtle*:

The turtle lives 'twixt plated decks
Which practically conceal its sex.
I think it clever of the turtle
In such a fix to be so fertile.

The Chinese Communist leader Mao Zedong (1893–1976) was also a poet. In 1937 he wrote:

In the land of China,
The nine-bedded river, the Yang Tse Kiang.
This shifting barrier
Divides the land, the North from the South . . .
The Serpent and the Tortoise
Watch one another ages without end . . .
While I, a wandering poet, let my gaze
Fall earthwards from the height of the tower.

The reference to the serpent and the tortoise is to two promontories on the river that represented the two different worlds of Northern and Southern China. In 1956 Mao wrote:

But the Serpent and the Tortoise
Keep their endless watch

And visions of times to come
Rise before my eyes . . .
From the South bank to the North
Men will throw a bridge of iron.
They will forget that once was here
An impassable chasm.[15]

The bridge was completed in 1957, uniting China eight years after the Communist victory ended the age-old scourge of the warlords.

In her comic novel *Cold Comfort Farm* (1932), Stella Gibbons made an apt comparison on attitude:

Turning from the taxi to the house, she saw that the door had already been opened by Mrs Smiling's butler, Sneller, who was looking down upon her with dim approval. He was, she reflected, almost *rudely* like a tortoise; and she was glad her friend kept none as pets or they might have suspected mockery.[16]

The British Chelonia Group Newsletter recorded the aspirations:

May My Life Be Like A Tortoise

As I walk through life, may my steps be like those of a tortoise, sure and steady.

No matter what obstacle is placed in his path, he will eventually find a way round, over or under it.

And if any unthinking person should pick him up and put him down again facing the opposite way, he will always turn round, find his original path, and head for his ultimate goal.

May I be covered like the tortoise with a hard, round, waterproof shell, to protect me from the knocks and bruises of life and give me shelter from the storms, and should I ever fall flat on my back, may a friend always be there to turn me gently on my feet again.

May my skin be like that of a tortoise, thick and leathery, so that harsh words spoken in anger will not pierce my heart.

May my heart be like the legs and claws of a tortoise, sturdy and strong, and no matter how hard, dry or stony the ground may be, I shall always be able to dig in it and plant the seeds of happiness, peace and contentment, and may all the seeds that I plant in my life grow and flower and bear wondrous fruits.

And lastly, may my eyes be like those of the tortoise, shiny and bright, never looking back at the storm clouds gathered behind, but always looking ahead to a bright and shiny future.

With luck, tortoises could bring that. Staff at Longleat wildlife park in Wiltshire, where the Mediterranean spur-thighed species is bred, paint numbers on their shells. The first six to emerge from their shelter on a Saturday morning provide the numbers for entry in the National Lottery draw in the evening.

Psychologists argue that tortoises have an almost instinctive appeal to children because the shell offers a safe retreat and represents security. Their slow, ambling gait is in no way threatening. Similarly, tortoises lend themselves to children's literature, yet, considering the number of tortoises that were kept as pets, the references are comparatively few. In *The Tale of Jeremy Fisher*, Beatrix Potter (1866–1943) introduced a minor character at the dinner: 'And Mr Alderman Ptolemy Tortoise brought a salad with him in a string bag.' Ruth Ainsworth wrote *The Ten Tales of Shellover* (1963), which became a children's paperback. In the USA the writer and illustrator Dr Seuss produced *Yertle the Turtle* (1958); and *Old Turtle* (1992), Douglas Wood's environmentally friendly fable, was the American Booksellers Association Book of the Year for 1993 and won the Children's Book Award of the International Reading Association. In *Snow White and the Seven Dwarfs* (1937), Walt Disney's first full-length animated feature, the tortoise had only a minor role. An East German animated film of 1985, *Die Schildkröte hat Geburtstag* (The Tortoise Has a Birthday), based on a story by Elizabeth Shaw, celebrated a 100th birthday. The Zoo Man, a regular speaker on the BBC radio programme *Children's Hour* from 1934 to 1945, also answered listeners' letters. Pet tortoises made regular appearances on the BBC children's TV series *Blue Peter*, which began in 1958. Among the menagerie of puppet characters for younger viewers of Bill and Ben the Flowerpot Men was a tetchy tortoise named Slowcoach. The creatures lend themselves to animation, as in a series like *Bob the Builder*.

In *Hunt the Tortoise* (1950), a detective story by Elizabeth Ferrars, Zizi, a tortoise pet, plays a diversionary role. Zizi is 'lost' in the garden so that people go looking for her, enabling the murderer to make a crucial telephone call from inside the hotel. In Ruth Rendell's *Live Flesh* (1986), Victor, on the eve of his seventh birthday, discovers his parents copulating, and immediately afterwards finds his birthday present, a tortoise, hidden in the larder. This traumatic event is 'the primal scene' of his life. From that moment Victor, who became a rapist, had a phobia about the creatures, the sight of even inanimate representations causing him to faint. He avoided pet shops and awoke from nightmares featuring them, screaming in agony and fear.

A tortoise was one of the animals of Coconino County that encountered Krazy Kat created by strip cartoonist George Herriman III (1880–1944) when he worked for William Randolph Hearst's *New York Journal American*. Herriman based Coconino County on the US South-West.

Alan Bennett's play *Kafka's Dick* (1986) is based on the premise that its hero did not die of TB in 1924. Like the character in his most famous story, *Metamorphosis,* who woke up as a beetle, Bennett's Kafka metamorphosed from a tortoise in the home of a minor English insurance official, Sydney. The play is an amusing debate about the writer's life involving Kafka, his domineering father Hermann, his faithful/faithless biographer Max Brod, Sydney and his literally minded wife. The dick of the title refers to Kafka's sensitivity about the size of his penis. Because a tortoise cannot be relied upon to perform on cue, a mechanical model is generally used in stage productions.

The Tortoise Shell (1996), a first novel by 72-year-old Fanny Frewen, has parallel stories. Heraclitus, named after the ancient Greek whose basic philosophy was 'All is flux', is cared for by Lady Lucy Dormer, who asks its opinion. When Heraclitus is run over, his shell damaged beyond repair, Lucy asks him to be put to sleep and he dies in her arms. His life in the village is paralleled by 95-year-old Cecilia, whom Lucy cannot bear to see suffer the indignity of having to leave her home, sold over her head by her daughter, to whom Lucy's husband had given power of attorney. Lucy, while being a night companion to Cecilia, gives her an overdose of sleeping tablets.

This was surely not the end of the tortoise in literature or art on a larger scale. As the range and scope of the media expand there is no reason why the role of the tortoise should not grow as well. It is helped by the concern for the care of the creatures, a movement that has been growing since the mid-twentieth century.

6 Conservation

After the Second World War concern for our fellow creatures was increased. People had been appalled at the depths of man's inhumanity to man, the treatment extending to genocide through industrialized murder. There was also a post-war disillusion with grand solutions, the idea that a particular 'ism' could solve a whole host of problems. During the 1950s attention turned increasingly to single issues about which individuals felt that they could do something. For instance, in 1952 the high-society ladies of Philadelphia organized a charity tortoise race on behalf of the city's distressed animals, the ladies parading in their hats and showing off their pets on leads. A 'steed of lightning' won.

On a wider scale the World Federation for the Protection of Animals was founded in 1953, and in 1959 the International Society for the Protection of Animals. Among all the good causes in developed countries was a growing minority seeking greater respect for tortoises, which were often regarded as expendable.

'Is the further importation of these doomed creatures really necessary?', asked Anthony Evans, editor of *The Aquarist and Pondkeeper*, in a letter to *The Times* of 2 June 1951. His question was prompted by the recent discovery of some 1,500 dead tortoises in baskets on the foreshore at Barking, Essex. The RSPCA had asked for a ban on imports at least during the hibernation period, when the animals were most likely to die, but the president of the Board of Trade had no power to do so. The most that the RSPCA could do was through the media and its own efforts, for instance through lectures in schools, to try to educate the public in proper care and treatment. Such efforts were of some value, as shown by the number of enquiries received by the reptile department of London Zoo when tortoises refused to hibernate. This occurred in mild autumn weather that was not cold enough to send them to sleep but in which they moved about, thus consuming their stock of food and energy stored during the summer. The answer was to put them in a covered but not airtight box in a cold place protected from frost and light.

The Universities Federation for Animal Welfare collected evidence on imports, which were measured in tons. When Morocco halved its annual tonnage of exports from 100 tons to 50, British importers looked elsewhere, buying from the Balkans and Tunisia. Whereas Balkan consignments were packed in well-ventilated boxes and transported in ventilated railway wagons that came directly to the UK in four or five days, Tunisian tortoises came as deck cargo from Tunis to Marseilles and then by train across France. As many as a half of them died. Some experts reckoned that only 1 per cent of imports survived for more than a year; the RSPCA was convinced that it was less than 10 per cent. One suggested way of reducing mortality was to prohibit the importation of tortoises less than four inches (10.16 cm) along the length of the under-shell.[1]

In 1962 the Federation supported a private members' bill to that effect presented to Parliament. Its outcome was a voluntary agreement by the importers to stop importing small tortoises, which did reduce the numbers brought into the UK from 189,000 in 1962 to 156,000 in 1963.[2] It was a temporary decrease. The Animals (Restriction of Importation) Act of 1964 made no difference. In the first half of 1972 the number had risen to 240,000. A similar number were imported into France, mainly from North Africa.[3]

The collection, packing and transport caused the creatures distress. Collection was often done by village children, who received the equivalent of pence for each animal. At packing centres they were kept without food and water to prevent defecation during transport. Some, crammed into wicker baskets, died from suffocation, starvation or crushing on route. A shipper's argument for dense packing was the prevention of damage. Shallow crates, not always as strongly made for stacking in refrigerated trucks as they ought to be, were designed so that on their long journeys tortoises would not climb on one another and could sleep. Their comatose state was similar to hibernation but could be mistaken for death, as it was in 1978 by BBC Television, which broadcast a libel on a tortoise importer, Robert Baltrock from Surrey, who had imported 42,000 tortoises from Turkey in refrigerated lorries. In 1982 the High Court awarded him substantial damages and costs. Counsel for the BBC said: 'The belief that many of the tortoises were dead was supported by the presence of a few dead tortoises in the crates.' It was accepted that these were not the result of neglect by the importer.[4]

The fate of consignments was occasionally made known to the public through the media by the RSPCA, which maintained special quarters at Harrow and a hostel at Heathrow Airport and had inspectors at ports. Incidents such as a cargo in 1972 of 1,400 Turkish tortoises dead and dying on a Greek ship after four weeks at sea led to calls in the House of Lords for a total ban on imports.[5]

What went unrecorded was the fate of the individual tortoises that survived their stressful journey and were then inadequately cared for in thousands of homes. One suggested remedy was a heavy Customs and Excise duty that would make the creatures sufficiently expensive to make it worthwhile looking after them properly. Cases of cruelty, such as boys stoning tortoises or breaking their shells, or a Japanese chef in the City of London failing to decapitate a tortoise and then plunging it live into boiling water, sometimes ended up in court and attracted condemnation.[6] Fines were small: in 1978, £50 for the Japanese chef and £25 for the head chef; fines on each of two livestock dealers for causing unnecessary suffering to a consignment of tortoises in transit reduced on appeal from £1,800 to £370.[7] The creatures could also be attacked by dogs, especially Jack Russells and terriers, foxes and badgers. Neglect went largely unnoticed.

In 1972 the Government did not consider that total prohibition of imports was justified, falling back on its intention to ratify a Council of Europe convention for the protection of animals during transit. Tortoiseshell fared better. From the beginning of 1976 there were new controls on the import and export of raw or unmade up items in the material. Attitudes were beginning to change. In 1979 it was reported that more than 6,000 tortoises were being bred on a 0.6 hectare farm near Nottingham, where the weather conditions were thought to be good for mating.[8] An importer had started the venture because of high casualties among imported tortoises. At the end of the year tortoise importers agreed to place a voluntary quota of 100,000 on the number of the animals entering Britain.[9] In France the sale of live tortoises as food by fishmongers was prohibited on health grounds. Tortoises are known to carry zoonoses, diseases transmissible between animals and humans. A high proportion of their faeces contains strains of salmonella, and owners, especially children, are advised to wash their hands thoroughly after handling the creatures. In the USA trade between some states is forbidden.

Importation of Mediterranean tortoises, mainly of the Spur-thighed species, into the UK and other countries had been carried on since the 1890s. After the Second World War, when stocks in North Africa were dwindling, Eastern Europe became another source, of the Hermann's and Marginated species. From 1984 the European Economic Community imposed a ban on these three species of tortoise: Spur-thighed, Hermann's and Marginated. This regulation, 3626/82, was in accordance with Appendix 1 of the Convention for International Trade in Endangered Species (CITES) prohibiting their commercial trade. It was estimated that over nearly a century more than 10 million of the creatures had been imported into the UK alone, only one million surviving their first year of captivity.

To bring the regulation to the notice of international travellers, a Buyer Beware exhibition at airports was organized by the World Wide Fund for Nature and HM Customs and Excise. The ban did not mean that Mediterranean tortoises could no longer be obtained, because they were being bred in captivity. Giving them away without gain in money or goods is not illegal. Their sale, barter or exchange, however, required a licence, in the UK from the Wildlife and Trade Licensing Branch of the Department of the Environment. Unfortunately, the forms that breeders were asked to fill in to accompany each creature that was sold were all too easy to duplicate.

Illegal imports seized by HM Customs were rehoused with responsible owners through chelonian societies. This happened, for example, when Russian seamen recently tried to barter 22 tortoises at Gatwick Airport in exchange for cigarettes. Seeing the shop assistant's horrified expression, the Russians fled, also leaving behind among potted plants five chameleons. Two

Egyptian sailors were caught trying to sell rare specimens in the marketplace at Cleethorpes, Lincolnshire. The sailors, who claimed that the creatures were good luck charms, went to jail for four months while the tortoises went to the Tortoise Trust.

The tortoises were Egyptian, an endangered species. Their desert habitats are being destroyed by tourism developments, the increasing herds of grazing sheep and goats, land reclamation schemes and modern agricultural methods. Bedouins now transport their herds in trucks from one grazing site to another, including marginal areas, causing severe over-grazing. There is direct competition for the same habitats, food items and feeding seasons. Woody scrub that is a natural home for the animals is also a traditional building material for Bedouin semi-permanent structures. New irrigation techniques and the cultivation of drought-resistant crops such as peach trees in north Sinai annex tortoise territory. Unlike ploughing with camels, donkeys and simple implements, machinery indiscriminately destroys perennial vegetation.

As if these accelerating developments were not enough, there are also natural enemies to contend with. Being small, at two months weighing only 10 grams, Egyptian tortoises fall prey to crows, ravens, wolves, hyenas and foxes. Sheltering in a burrow from the desert heat, they come up against rodents. Being rare, the tortoises can command a price. A police raid on the notorious Saiyyida Aisha animal market in Cairo in February 1997 led to the confiscation of more than 300 Egyptian tortoises, many of them in poor condition, suffering from dehydration and pneumonia. An international effort was mounted to provide immediate care and secure their long-term future. Captive-bred and fitted with radio transmitters so that they can be tracked, they are now being reintroduced into their country of origin in an area protected under a conservation

The tiny Egyptian tortoise, which rarely reaches more than 15 cm in length, appeals through the bold contrast of its markings, seen here in an 1880s French scientific illustration.

plan. Humans make the biggest adverse impact on tortoise life and only they can rectify that.[10]

The principal consequence of the ban was to make the most common species of tortoise within the ten and all future member states of the European Economic Community a rarer item. Scarcity made them more valuable, especially after the poor summer of 1985, when many had been less active, eating insufficient food and building up inadequate fat reserves to sustain them through the longer hibernation out of their natural habitat. Creatures that had cost a few shillings in the 1950s were now quoted in three figures, an inflation rate greater than on property and comparable with the increase in value of certain items of art. In 1986 the British Chelonia Group, an organization set up to protect the creatures, warned that tortoises were being stolen and sold for up to £150. Money was not the crucial issue. Owners who had had them as pets for years were distressed at losing them, and were concerned that whoever had taken them would not look after them properly as the family had done. There was resentment that their pets had probably been sold in places like pubs to pay for a drink or drugs habit.

In 1999 Tracey Lewis, who had been holidaying at a North Wales campsite, saw a tortoise wandering in the middle of a road and picked it up to stop it being run over. Not knowing where it was from, she put it in woodland near the site to fend for itself. A week later she was traced through a private detective, hired by its owners to gather information on missing Terry, their 'heirloom', who had been in the family for 42 years. Police arrested and detained Tracey for seven hours before, to her disbelief, she was interviewed on a charge of a £600 theft. A couple who had found Terry in the woods returned him to his owners and the case against Tracey was dropped.[11]

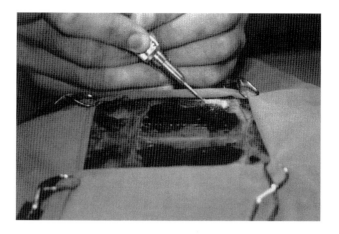

Injecting an identifying microchip smaller than a grain of rice is a delicate operation.

When tortoise rustlers were around, painting an address on the shell was less of an inducement for a wanderer of increasing value to be returned. By 1999 a reward of £500 was being offered for the return of Sammy, a pet of 37 years stolen from a Kent garage. He could have been more valuable than some of the tools that were also stolen. National and local publicity was organized, informing members of chelonian societies, the police, RSPCA, vets and the pet trade. Five months after being stolen, Sammy was recovered through an anonymous telephone caller stating where he could be collected. Bonnie and Clyde, taken from a garden shed in Lingfield, Surrey, were valued by the family at £4,000. A thief in the north-east of England released a tortoise, a pet for 45 years, by burning through the nylon rope that tethered it. Better security became necessary. One way was to protect their quarters with burglar alarms.

The sharp increase in prices encouraged smuggling of creatures from the wild. In their home countries tortoises are comparatively cheap, often no more than the equivalent of 2 euros, good money for children and other locals who gather them. Dealers in markets think so little of them that they keep them in cages in hot sunlight with little food and water. In the *souks* of tourist cities such as Marrakesh in Morocco, where sheep's heads are openly on view and baby tortoises for sale are crammed in baskets, merchants aware of hostile opinion towards their trade stand in front of would-be photographers to prevent them getting convincing evidence. For export the creatures are crammed into boxes and suitcases. Sale in Europe can net profits of at least one hundredfold. No wonder the trade, which had been declining, is once more on the increase. In August 2000 Italian police intercepted at Rome airport a consignment of 20,000 banned red cheek tortoises imported from Louisiana, USA. An endangered species found in North America and Asia, the tiny tortoises, only a few days old and the size of a coin, had been crammed into 40 cardboard boxes. The Turin dealer, who had bought the animals for around $1 each, faced criminal charges.

With increase in value, more sophisticated methods of identification were necessary. Since the underside of the shell is unique in colour and pattern and remains so even with growth, a photograph of it is as good as a human fingerprint. The 'fingerprint' is translated into a computer image, to which can be added for a register details such as breed, age and other distinguishing marks. A more sophisticated and costly method is to have a microchip fitted by a vet. This is an invasive procedure of injecting a tiny device into the animal's skin, the recommended site being the left hind leg. The neck or shoulder area is not recommended because of the risk of lacerating the jugular vein or carotid artery. Microchips are rather large for tortoises under ten years old, especially smaller breeds. Injection has been compared to inserting a mobile phone in the human groin. The size of a chip makes impractical the well-intentioned

EC Regulations 338/97 and 939/97 that hatchlings cannot be sold without a personalized microchip. There is also the risk that a chip may move around the animal's body and cause infection. A microchip cannot be removed and is a 'permanent' way of marking and identifying individual creatures. How 'permanent' in the lifespan of a tortoise is unknown. The chip is read by a hand-held scanner.

Not only family pets were at risk. In 1999 two tiny and rare Egyptian tortoises were stolen from the Bronx Zoo during the weekly 'free day'. Thieves used a screwdriver to lift the edge of a heavy plate glass cover, reached in and grabbed the 6.3-centimetre-long creatures, worth $500–600 each on the black market. They were the first that the zoo had hatched in captivity, under carefully controlled desert-like conditions, following the international agreement to ban their commercial sale from 1995, when there were believed to be fewer than 5,000 in existence. Fortunately, a Bronx man saw two late teenagers playing with the tortoises in a nearby park, offered them $90 for the pair, which was accepted, saw a television news report about the theft and phoned the police, who arranged their return to the zoo. In future they would be protected by security cameras.[12]

The European ban on importation led to much more interest in breeding and the raising of hatchlings, which take about 72 days to emerge from their eggs, attention to their living conditions, diet, and a knowledge of their diseases and treatment. Advice is given in articles, leaflets, talks and videos. In the UK the national bodies are The British Chelonia Group, formed in 1976, and The Tortoise Trust (1986), a branch of the world's largest tortoise and turtle organization with members in more than 26 countries. There are zoos and also local societies. Interest is international. For instance, the California Turtle and Tortoise Club has been 'dedicated to turtle and tortoise preservation, conservation, study and education since 1964'. It publishes the monthly *Tortuga Gazette* of educational information. Another group specializes in the desert tortoise. International symposia are held on conservation and captive husbandry, with action plans as the outcome. Reports on trade in certain areas, for example, India and South-East Asia, are published. Care and conservation are the essence of current publications.

Within clubs there is mutual help. Incubation services are offered by members on condition that the hatchlings are not sold; matches of sex and species are arranged. Particular care has to be given to hatchlings, which at birth weigh only 5–15 grams. For their first few years they are not strong enough to hibernate through a winter longer than would have been natural to them. They need to be kept in a vivarium, ideally in a thermostatically controlled environment with appropriate day and night temperatures. Their colourful salads, in reasonable quantities, should be sprinkled with vitamin/mineral supplements. Overfeeding, though, can lead to hatchlings becoming overweight when their carapace is still soft and forming. As a result it sets too low, producing too deep a shell that makes it difficult for the creature to move. Advice is also given on sexing and identifying particular species, which should not be mixed. In their own form of tribal warfare they can bite one another.

There are many factors in proper care to consider. Is a garden secure against escape and free of poisonous plants? If eaten, slug pellets can be fatal, as can goose droppings. Tortoises are better climbers than most people imagine. They can hibernate naturally but not necessarily safely, digging themselves well down in the soil or concealing themselves in garden rubbish piled for a bonfire. Unintentional cremation can occur and the creatures are also at the mercy of predators unearthing them. They are better off in a cool indoor environment, ideally about

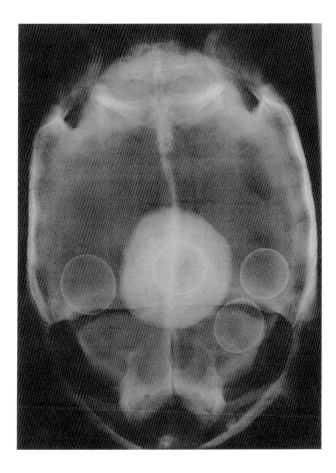

Like human beings, tortoises can suffer from a build-up of stone in the bladder, shown on the x-ray.

4°c, but this too must be safe. There are instances of rats invading sheds and leaving an empty shell to be discovered in the spring. Winter sleep should be in suitable insulating material. Hay and straw are not recommended because they may be infested with mites or cause respiratory problems. Clean shredded paper is better.

This x-ray reveals the patient is egg-bound.

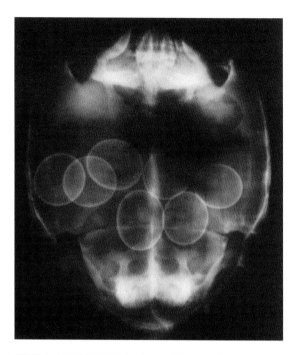

Key-hole surgery is performed through the plastron.

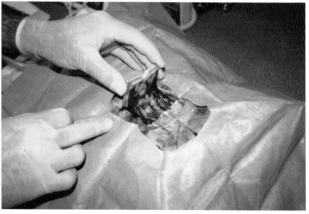

The eggs are removed.

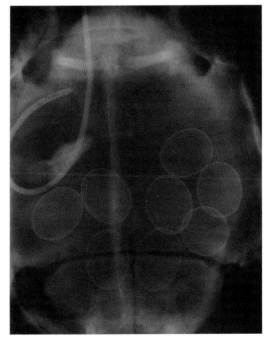

Egg-bound tortoises lose appetite, causing fat reserves to be absorbed into the bloodstream, damaging the liver. Part of the treatment for an anorexic tortoise is a high-fibre diet administered directly into the stomach.

This Horsefield hatchling, with a comparatively soft shell, was attacked by a dog.

Acrylic resin was used to bond several parts of the shell together again, enabling the hatchling to survive and grow.

After surgery, cuts in the shell are sealed with acrylic resin and protected with a dressing. In time the shell heals completely.

After 25 years walking on three legs, Hoppy had worn his plastron so thin it was traumatizing his soft tissue. A mini-skateboard raises him to an even height, and the wheels can easily be removed when he is not on a hard surface.

Today animal transport is much more rapid. These tortoises, at the Animal Reception Centre in London's Heathrow Airport, have been air-freighted in specially designed boxes.

Most diseases in tortoises are caused by poor environment and nutrition. Bacterial, fungal, viral and parasitic infections can affect the shell, and require veterinary treatment. If left untreated for too long, the shell can become permanently distorted. Burns from bonfires and other sources also need expert treatment. Ticks can often be removed with tweezers. Claws not worn down in moving around gardens without rocks may need clipping. Intestinal worms are treated with drugs. When there are problems in reproduction, for example the presence of abnormal eggs, detected by ultrasound or x-ray, that cannot be removed medically, a Caesarean operation can be performed under anaesthetic. For access, a high-powered surgical saw is used to cut a square flap out of the shell. On completion, the flap is replaced. Shell damaged by an attack from a dog, a fox or a rat or a blow, accidentally or purposely, can be repaired with glass fibre, which will be sloughed off when the shell re-grows. Unlike our fingernails, the shell is a living organism.

In 1998 a veterinary surgeon rebuilt a shell that had been smashed into 30 pieces by two 10-year-old boys with a brick. It was a painstaking two-day operation in which any pieces that had come away from the body could not be used and the rest had to be cleaned against infection and straightened to heal under a bandage. After losing or breaking a leg in a fall, tortoises have been fitted with a child's toy car wheel. An alternative, claimed to offer better balance, is to fit disabled tortoises with their own Zimmer frame, a base and four wheels. The frame is fixed to the underside of the tortoise with a strong adhesive and the wheels have independent suspension to help cornering. Such an operation, professionally performed, can benefit tortoises with spinal injuries and those that have been overfed as hatchlings. Three screws, two in the lower jaw and one in the upper, and a strong rubber band were the remedy for the misaligned jaw of Cynthia, a 25-kilogram Burmese tortoise at Taronga Zoo Education Centre in Sydney, Australia. The rubber band, acting as a brace, was removed regularly for feeding. Tortoises, which are unable to cough, can suffer from respiratory diseases such as pneumonia.

The European Community ban also applied to tortoiseshell. From 1 January 1984 it was illegal to import, buy or sell tortoiseshell unless the object was imported or made before that date. One specialized business to suffer was the manufacture of violin and cello bows. Tortoiseshell formed the nut, the block that connects the horsehair with the stick, and fastidious buyers were not keen on a synthetic substitute.

Prohibition was not universal and not always easy to police. Ann Ovenstone, a British visitor to Tunisia in 1997, saw in Sousse:

an absolute mountain of at least 300 tortoise shells, all neatly stacked up like car tyres and all identical, about 4 inches long, beautifully marked and selling for £6.00 each. But the biggest horror was on the shelves behind the cash-out, row upon row of beautifully coloured tortoises, bright yellow markings on legs and head still only about 4 inches long, preserved in several coats of yacht varnish. I was later to discover that these tortoises are either forcibly drowned by being wedged under water or held over on their backs until dead. They are then manipulated into the required position and then dipped a few times in a vat of varnish and left to dry. These were selling for £12.00 and judging by the amount on offer they must be a good tourist line. In the casbahs and souks behind the shops which contain hundreds of stalls that went like a maze in and out of the old walled town, I estimated that one in every four stalls were selling live tortoises. At the first stall I bent over the cardboard box crammed with about two dozen of the animals and picked one up, it was pitifully underweight and lethargic and in a very sorry state. Of course, the owner seeing a potential buyer was out like a flash, and I was dragged into the back room only to be presented with yet another box containing 20 or so hatchlings about 1½ inches long and was informed that they were seven days old and would fit nicely into the pocket to take home, make me an offer! was the price.[13]

The tortoise trade in Europe has by no means ended. It is still possible to buy in pet stores locally bred species not regarded as endangered, for instance leopard and Indian star tortoises. They do make suitable pets in families where there are allergies to more common animals such as cats and dogs.

In South-East Asia tortoises were still being exploited for food and medicinal purposes, and to a lesser extent the pet trade, as revealed by surveys of 1993–5 conducted by TRAFFIC, the wildlife monitoring programme of the World Wide Fund for Nature and The World Conservation Union. The trade was growing rapidly and included hundreds of thousands of tortoises annually. They came from Burma, Cambodia and Laos and found their way, often being smuggled, via Vietnam to China, for use in traditional medicine. They might find their way as an ingredient into curative tea, claimed to be a heat reliever, to ease diuresis, lessen itching on the skin, even ameliorate complaints as serious as eczema and psoriasis. Estimates of the trade were around 150,000–300,000 kilograms annually, with a minimum value of $1 million. Low carriage costs and high profit margins have made the reptile trade a lucrative business while bringing many species to the brink of extinction. Via international smuggling rings, endangered species can reach as far as the USA.

Eggs as well as meat are in demand. Islamic dietary restrictions forbid the eating of tortoise flesh but this does not apply to eggs, which are highly esteemed in many Muslim areas. One saving grace is Buddhist influence. Sending a tortoise to a temple, thus preventing it from being eaten, is an act of saving a life and one that will be rewarded in the person's next incarnation.

As well as prohibition, determined efforts have been made at conservation, especially of endangered species. The appropriately named Charles Darwin Research Station was established on Santa Cruz Island to protect the Galapagos giant tortoises, of which there are fourteen surviving sub-species. Naming the station after Darwin was doubly appropriate, because as a young man he had researched on Galapagos and in his later years worked with other conservationists and the governor of Mauritius to establish a captive breeding population of Aldabra giant tortoises on Mauritius, as well as protecting the

Through Darwin's influence, tortoises were rescued from Aldabra and taken south to the island of Mauritius, where they continue to flourish.

Aldabra Atoll. Captive breeding and study of the reptile should ensure its continued survival. Supported by the Galapagos Conservation Trust, founded in 1995, progress has been remarkable. For example as reported in *Galapagos News*, on 24

Espèces menacées d'extinction F.S. 0,90

Nations Unies

Geochelone elephantopus (Tortue géante des îles Galapagos) Higgins Bond (2001)

Galapagos tortoises were among the endangered species featured in a United Nations stamp series in 2001.

March 2000, the one thousandth tortoise was released on its native island of Espanola, where in mid-1963 a single animal was found eating a cactus pad surrounded by fifteen munching goats. Moreover, it was isolated from its few fellow creatures and might not easily find them to breed. All the goats have since been removed from Espanola.

A similar project exists in the Seychelles. A local custom was to give newborn girls a baby tortoise to be eaten fully grown at the wedding feast. When Queen Elizabeth II was given a pair of giants from the Seychelles they were passed on to a zoo for proper care. Aldabra has been designated a World Heritage Site and its tortoises have appeared on Seychelles coins and notes. On the privately owned Bird Island, a large male, Esmeralda, reputed to be 150 years old, gives rides to children. A British couple on a return visit thoughtfully brought him a bag of lettuce. One thing that has to be watched in moving tortoises to secure locations is that diseases or potentially dangerous organisms are not being introduced into healthy populations. Protection of the giant tortoises of Changuu Island, Zanzibar, against poachers has been made easier by the use of microchips.

At risk is the pancake tortoise of East Africa. This species, with its soft, flexible shell, has the unique knack of being able to scurry under boulders and into fissures when it is threatened. Pancake tortoises tend to keep close to their refuge because their soft shells make them vulnerable to birds of prey, such as the ground hornbill, or small carnivores, such as mongooses and civet cats. Even more at risk is the ploughshare tortoise of Madagascar, so-called from the horn protruding at the front of its under-shell. It is the world's rarest tortoise and only some 400 are thought to be in existence. So prized are they by collectors that half the total captive population was stolen from their compound in the Madagascar jungle.

France, with the will and the climate, has led Europe in providing tortoise sanctuaries, notably on the island of Corsica. Starting in 1985 with one Hermann tortoise wounded by a dog, an accountant, Philippe Magnan, who as a child had two tortoises, Zoa and Zoé, has gone on to realize a boyhood dream of breeding, studying and protecting his favourite creature. On a 2.5-hectare area near the Corsican capital Ajaccio, with the help of friends he has established an association and site, A Cupulatta, which he claims is Europe's premier sanctuary for chelonians. Here they can enjoy a natural environment in a favourable Mediterranean climate. There were already tortoises there and the population now numbers some 3,000 tortoises, turtles and terrapins of more than 150 species from five continents, attracting more than 50,000 visitors a year. It was opened to the public in 1998.

On the mainland, to protect the most endangered reptile of France, the Hermann's tortoise, SOPTOM (Station d'Observation et de Protection de Tortues des Maures) was established in 1988 in the natural surroundings of the foothills of the Massif des Maures. This is a specially constructed tortoise village in the

Alpes de Haute Provence in which all the animals have been donated by their former owners and are being cared for before being released to re-populate the area. Success there has led to the establishment of similar centres in the Vallée des Tortues near Perpignan, close to the Pyrenees, and in the Asco valley of northern Corsica, part of the Parque Nationale. In 2000 a website was established where visitors can seek information and advice. In south-west Turkey at the Olympos Village, Tortoise Sanctuary hatchlings are raised to be released into the wild when they are five years old. The French lead has been followed in Francophone West Africa with the establishment of Le Centre de Protection des Tortues du Senegal.

American Tortoise Rescue was founded in 1990 in Malibu, California, by a husband-and-wife team, Susan Tellem and Marshall Thompson, to rescue, rehabilitate, adopt and protect all species of tortoise and turtle, creatures that many people regard as 'rocks with legs'. Summer months are their busiest times for rescue. Many of the creatures rescued are injured or ill. Problems range from dog bites and other predator attacks, being run over by cars, amputations, shell rot, starvation, stress, failure to thrive, upper respiratory infections, parasites, worms and other medical problems such as liver and kidney diseases. Many of the conditions are caused by owners or ignorant individuals. Some are cruelty cases.

Along with Tortoise Trust USA, American Tortoise Rescue warns the public against purchasing sulcata hatchlings, the most commonly purchased pet tortoise in North America. Natives of sub-Saharan Africa, sulcatas develop into giant tortoises, the third largest species in the world. Adult females can produce as many as 90 eggs a year, and, in a comparatively short time, especially if generously fed as pets, the hatchlings can attain a weight of 100 kilograms. Along with the weight goes strength and aggression. Darrell Senneke, director of Tortoise Trust USA, warned: 'New owners quickly become aware of the difficulties associated with having a potentially destructive non-housebroken animal of this size. A fully-grown sulcata can easily move a piano or walk through a typical house or apartment wall.' Susan Tellem added: 'Many owners assume that when the tortoise becomes a problem zoos will take them. This is simply not true. Zoos are not interested in cast-off pets' (joint Press release, 1 May 2001). Rescue sites can take only a few of them.

Dedicated to the study and conservation of tortoises and turtles is the Florida-based Chelonian Research Institute, founded in 1997. Its director, Dr Peter Pritchard, author of *Encyclopedia of Turtles* (1979), *The Galápagos Tortoises* (1996) and scientific and popular articles, outlined the Institute's resources:

We have gathered a varied collection of live creatures, including Aldabra and Galapagos tortoises, and preserved specimens, both in alcohol and skeletonised. The collection has been built up through my own worldwide travels and by donations. No creatures have ever been sacrificed to provide either preserved specimens or skeletons for the Institute. Along with our scientific library, map, slide, film and video collections and an eclectic assortment of relevant artwork ranging from classical engravings to contemporary original art, posters and curiosities, they constitute an international resource for visiting scientists and students. We also carry out fieldwork abroad.

Experts from various Western institutes and zoos visit native habitats to provide husbandry and management advice on matters of health and security. They collect information on aspects of behaviour, organize surveys of habitat areas to determine population trends, advise on the establishment of refuges, breeding, research and public education programmes. Visits are usually no more than a few weeks or months at most, but the important thing is to leave behind local conservationists who will carry on the work and keep in contact.

There is still a conflict between wild life and 'progress'. Tortoises favour coastal heathlands, natural habitat wanted for commercial developments such as villas in Greece, deliberately fired for land clearance, invaded by the drivers of dune buggies and motor cycle scramblers. Building on the sandy habitats of gopher tortoises in Florida, the Sunshine State, brings twin hazards. More people means more cars, which can kill or maim the creatures. Discarded food attracts raccoons, which in turn eat both tortoise eggs and newly hatched babies. Tortoises mature slowly, produce relatively few young each year and have a high juvenile mortality rate, so recovery of depleted populations takes some time. Other areas are taken over for agriculture and stock raising. Poachers in countries where incomes are low can obtain quick returns from collectors of rare and endangered species. Only occasionally are they caught.

It is a constant battle between high-minded conservationists thinking in terms of our worldwide natural heritage and the 'needs' of humans. Undoubtedly, conservationists have made considerable progress in the developed world, restricting trade and caring for existing creatures. Through the media there is much greater international awareness of endangered species. Native populations, however, see wild life as a commodity that can be turned into quantities of cash far above that to be made in primary production or everyday trade in basic items. In spite of successes in consignment seizures of endangered species and promising regeneration programmes, at times it seems an unequal battle. Across a gulf of cross purposes the war is not yet over.

7 Promotion

Comparatively rare, tortoise-shell bamboo is easily distinguished.

Drawing a tortoise is child's play, the result instantly recognizable. Its outline or silhouette, in artifice or nature, cannot be mistaken for any other creature. For instance, there is a Tortoise Rock formed by erosion at Castro Laboreiro in the Parque Nacional da Peneda-Gerês, north-west Portugal. Similarly, the indigenous inhabitants of Paarl in Western Cape Province, South Africa, knew the three large glistening granite outcrops as Tortoise Mountain. There is a rare variation of bamboo known as tortoise-shell simply because its surface looks like a series of tortoise shells.

With its distinctive shape, the creature has been represented in bath oil capsules, bookmarks, bottle stops, bread (sometimes full of canapés), candles, carved coconuts, in *cloisonné*, computer clip-art, doorstops and associated shoe brushes, on fabrics, fridge magnets, garden ornaments cast in cement (some of them nodding), on glasses, as haversacks, hobs, holders (e.g. for paper clips), keyrings, jelly moulds, jewellery such as pendants, lace, lamps (among them modern productions in the art nouveau style of the Tiffany Collection with mosaics of opalescent glass), mats (mouse, table, etc.), musical boxes, money boxes having a slit in the top, notebook covers, paperweights, pencil sharpeners and tops, puppets (the Pelham puppet of 1963 being a rare item among collectors), rings (the finger going through the body of

168

the tortoise), soap, sponges, stencils, T-shirts, tea caddies and pots, tea towels, ties, tiles, topiary, on tops of pens, as toys (mechanical and soft), weathervanes and in many other ways.

Without their top shell, tortoises are modelled as receptacles from ashtrays to plant pots. Adrian Fisher designed a maze of 1,600 yew trees at Edinburgh Zoo in 1995 in the shape of a Galapagos tortoise. In the USA, a turtleback was the name given to a rounded projection on the back of a vehicle or a raised obstruction, sometimes illuminated, placed in the pavement at a street intersection for the guidance of traffic.

In cartoons a tortoise represents one of the species' common attributes, typically age or slowness. Hence its popularity in

The distinctive shape and the appearance of the shell lend themselves to a modern lamp in the Tiffany style.

The Darwin Maze at Edinburgh Zoo – 'fun, fountains and fascinating facts about the theory of evolution'.

publications such as the British magazine *The Oldie*. It is a convenient way of making a generation comment, such as 'Young people today, they want it all now.' A *New Yorker* cartoon of two Galapagos tortoises talking has one saying to the other: 'Sure I remember Darwin. Nice fellow.' Delay, especially by officialdom, is portrayed by a tortoise as a messenger, sometimes bearing a stack of papers on his back.

Devotion to tortoises, especially by the elderly, is a favourite cartoon theme.

THE OLDIES   TONY HUSBAND

Oh that will be the Vet about our tortoise
I'll get it

BBRING

He's going to be O.K. fantastic, wonderful, wonderful

Dear God. I was only joking when I said take him or me

Greetings cards feature cheerful anthropomorphic creatures, usually smiling, perhaps waving, often with eyes popping. Raised bug eyes emphasize the point and make for extra sales. Jokes about getting older are popular in birthday cards, about which you can do nothing beyond accepting the fact and making the most of your time. Two young tortoises are sitting on bar stools, she peering down the front of his shell and asking the leading question: 'Your place or mine?'

Companies have employed tortoises in their advertising. Because the creature is instantly recognizable yet has so many different attributes it can be linked to a diverse range of products and services. It was one of the animal series created in 1936 by the artist John Gilroy for the brewers Guinness: 'Have a Guinness when you're tired.' *Do You Remember?*, a 12-minute newsreel-style production of 1951 by British Transport Films for London Transport, included Percy the tortoise left on a bus. Shown in London cinemas and made available to interested

Greetings cards use age as a theme. The inside of the one on the left reads 'What? Are you in some kind of hurry to get old?!'

Bosch used this image of a tortoise getting its skates on to promote a washing machine going 40 per cent faster with no loss of performance.

The Guinness tortoise advertisement from 1936 is still alive on drinking glasses, lapel badges, mouse mats, postcards and elsewhere.

Have a
GUINNESS
when you're
TIRED

In its promotion, Citroën likened its long-selling 2CV to a tortoise.

groups, it promoted use of the lost property office. In the 1960s the Gordon-Keeble car company in the UK paradoxically used a tortoise as its emblem for its high-performance cars, offering speeds up to 135 m.p.h. Unfortunately, it was more applicable to sales, which slowed as prices rose. Altogether the company

Rome has a gallery for civilized tortoise objects, a contrast to the crude and cruel trade in tortoises across the Mediterranean in North Africa.

made only 99 cars. Still, they have become classic models. A less sleek model, the Citroën 2cv, made from 1949 until 1990, was likened in the company's advertisements to a tortoise. In 2000 Fiat used the creature in TV advertisements to promote a car.

Car care was the inspiration of the inventive chemist Ben Hirsch, who formulated the world's first preparation of its kind, Plastone Liquid Car Polish, introduced in 1941. In the early 1950s, returning to Chicago from a business trip in Beloit, Wisconsin, he went through the small town of Turtle Creek. Noting the similarity between his product and the creature's protective shell, he renamed the polish Super Hard Shell® and his company TurtleWax®, with a happy, shiny tortoise as its mascot. Later in the 1950s the company made a landmark of its brand by erecting on top of its nine-storey headquarters in Chicago a 'Turtle in the Sky', a large clock and weather fore-caster. The tortoise still features in the company's promotional material, offering, for example in strip cartoons, car care tips using an enlarged range of products. Giving products a consis-tent personality has paid off in more than 60 countries.

Atop the head office of TurtleWax® in Chicago, the mascot forecasts weather.

On the ground he offers tips on car care.

Belgian bank BBL advertised its mortgages with the slogan 'Own house, nice house'.

A British Airways poster used the caption 'Your own cabin'. Insurance companies emphasize cover. In the 1970s the Scottish company General Accident had one tortoise advising another that the Maxplan was right for contents while the Economy was perfectly adequate for a house well above flood levels. Investment houses claim that tortoises can put on speed to regain ground from fast appreciating stocks. An HSBC advertisement featured the creature tying up his shoelaces and saying: 'I want a mortgage that's good value in the long run.' Home loans are promoted graphically by Banque Bruxelles Lambert in Belgium. In 1966, to compete with lighters, a Spanish matchmaker featured an alphabetical animal series of boxes, with the 'G' for Galapagos.

A link between electricity and tortoises developed in a roundabout way. Aardman Animations recorded various people's comments about zoos and then created plasticine animals to fit the voices. One interviewee who talked about being a very busy person and running to keep fit led to the idea of creating a tortoise. Frank the Tortoise, complete with sweatband, became a star of the Oscar-winning *Creature Comforts*, a hit with the public, and was adopted by the Electricity Council for its Heat Electric campaign. So memorable was Frank that he was later voted into the top five of all-time favourite TV commercials. More than ten years after his first appearance he returned to television screens with nearly 100 other animals in a series of ten-minute *Creature Comforts* films. For a British TV commercial, Cadbury's Caramel drew on the fable of the hare and the tortoise. The hare lost the race because it stopped to enjoy the Cadbury's product. A rival chocolate, Nestlé's KitKat, was promoted with a tortoise, emphasizing the theme of 'Have a break'.

On BBC TV the creature featured in the title of *One Foot in the Grave*, a sitcom about a crotchety pensioner, Victor Meldrew. The emblem warns golf club members to avoid slow play: 'Remember, your speed determines the speed of every group behind you for the rest of the day.' A local authority has used the creature as a street sign for promoting traffic calming, Motorola for its mobile phones. Friends of the Earth campaigners presented a golden tortoise to Tesco in 1999 as the only major British retailer that had not pledged to ban genetically modified foods from its shelves.

In 2000 the London opening of a comedy, *Cooking With Elvis*, was in doubt because of the unavailability of a trained tortoise to perform a crucial role at a reasonable price. At one point in the play Frank Skinner, the naked leading actor, had to grab Stanley the tortoise, who had walked across a table, and

A Slow Down road sign.

hold him in front of his privates. Having been quoted £270 a day for hiring a Stanley, the producer advertised in *The Stage* for a performing tortoise, offering a fee, warm accommodation, 'reasonable out-of-shell expenses', insurance and a six-month contract. One qualification was that the creature should like the music of Elvis Presley, but how a tortoise would demonstrate its interest in rock and roll at the audition was not clear. An owner of three candidates, each with a shining olive-oiled shell, claimed that they liked music, extrovertly listening to the radio with her when she was gardening. The whole affair was a clever publicity stunt in the month before the opening of the play. By the time that the RSPCA had objected to the use of a live tortoise in the performance and obliged the producer to use a cardboard replica, the promotion had done its work.

A badge or sticker of a tortoise with the letters GBS across the shell has nothing to do with George Bernard Shaw, who was both old and wise. It is Barry, the logo redrawn from computer clip-art and adopted originally for a new design of T-shirt in 1993 by the Guillain-Barré Syndrome Support Group of the United Kingdom. The disease, believed to be an allergic reaction to an infection, is a form of damage to the peripheral nervous system that causes weakness of the arms and legs. Weakness is often accompanied by numbness and tingling. It can become permanent or recur. Sufferers prefer to think GBS stands for Getting Better Slowly, an unofficial T-shirt slogan that has survived. Continuing the theme, a New Zealand support group uses the same artwork.

In an honourable tradition, tortoises have appeared on coins. A 15-shilling Elizabethan piece had a stylized tortoise climbing a palm tree. Large tortoises have a ready appeal, Galapagos types having appeared on coins of the Cook Islands and Ecuador, Seychelles on those of the islands themselves and St Helena, which has also honoured its resident Jonathan. Paper money has been issued by Madagascar featuring the radiated tortoise, the Seychelles with Aldabra examples and South Korea with a medieval tortoise warship. In 2001 an Aldabran, left during the First World War at the local zoo by a naval officer who did not return, was named The Admiral and made an honorary member of Durban naval base.

Along with their ancestors, turtles, tortoises are much more common on postage stamps, having been issued by more than 250 countries from Abakan in the northern part of the Russian Commonwealth by way of Denmark, Liechtenstein, Pitcairn Islands and the Vatican City to Zimbabwe in Southern Africa. Going back into prehistory, Israel issued in 1969 a stamp showing a tiny tortoise, too tiny to be seen with the naked eye, on the roof of a cabin of Noah's ark. They have also made their way on to phone cards from Brazil to Turkey, from China and the Czech Republic to the USA. The record number of appearances is in Japan. Like stamps, the cards are collectors' items.

In New South Wales, Australia, David H. Price is the principal of the Institute of Enterprising Tortoises and the Enterprising Tortoise business. A hare before he decided to become a tortoise, he regards the creatures as non-threatening, winsome, different and memorable. To them, the journey is more important than the destination. On his Internet website he states his stance:

The Tortoise Approach is an integrated, holistic process for transferring basic business skills and knowledge to people of all ages and stages in life. The overall aim is to provide packages and services that facilitate the growth and development of enterprise in both individuals and organisations. This unique approach empowers people to create and maintain a sustainable vision for their future and for the organisations to which they belong.

It sounds like life-long learning. To Price, passionate learning is about matching people with ideas. A fun process, it builds neural pathways that liberate and enable the toolbox between the ears to learn. Connecting people through ideas, he says, is the most effective and efficient way of developing knowledge. From this knowledge emerges a range of skills and attitudes. Back to the tortoise as a repository of ancient wisdom applicable today.

In a *Which?* survey of pets, tortoises scored low on entertainment value, a judgement with which many owners would disagree. They credit their pets with individual habits, sometimes including recognition of their owners and answering to their names when called. As pets they are not a nuisance as cats and dogs can be, especially to neighbours. A BANX cartoon has an oldish couple sitting in their front room, across which a tortoise is walking, the man remarking: 'It's funny how he's always my tortoise when he's been naughty.' They are not demanding creatures, exercising themselves in summer and then hibernating. Nor do they need grooming beyond occasional oil on the shell and trimming of claws that have grown too long away from the rougher terrain of their natural habitat. Feeding ideally on readily available natural greenstuff, they are not expensive to maintain. Their simple lifestyle is healthy, vets' bills only being high for specialized surgery. One complaint against them is that, unlike cats and dogs, they are incapable of showing affection, even to their young. They can, though, receive it, and enjoy being stroked on the head or under the chin.

After more than 200 million years, tortoises have entered the modern world. They have a number of sites on the Internet. Some are devoted to particular species, such as desert, gopher, radiated and red foot. They have their own picture galleries.

Other sites offer advice on their care, spell out international regulations, what is happening in conservation – American Tortoise Rescue, Dutch (and also Ontario) Turtle and Tortoise Society, Reno Tur-Toise Club, for example. Anti-smuggling has a website. One is fittingly called Slowcoach. After 200 million years the creature is still slow but sure, with a growing number of friends. Along with other pets, they may come to have a Bill of Rights. Meanwhile, they have their own international day, World Turtle Day, 23 May, the birthday of Carolus Linnaeus (1707–1778), the Swedish botanist and taxonomist who originated the modern scientific classification of plants and animals. The day is observed to help people celebrate and protect turtles and tortoises as well as their habitats around the world.

Timeline of the Tortoise

c. 225 MILLION BC	*c.* 200 MILLION BC	*c.* 1200–1045 BC	OLD TESTAMENT
In the Age of the Reptiles the first turtles and tortoises appear. Turtles emerge from water and develop on land as tortoises	With continental drift, the super-continent Pangaea splits up and tortoise species develop in different environments	Chinese divination using tortoise shells	According to Leviticus, the tortoise is an 'unclean creeping thing'

c. 300 BC	*c.* 80 BC	AD 4TH CENTURY	1420	16TH– 18TH CENTURIES
Bhagavad Gita cites the tortoise as an example of meditation for elevation to Krishna consciousness	The Roman craftsman Carvilius Pollio uses tortoise-shell for decorative purposes	St Jerome argues that the tortoise moves slowly because it is burdened with the weight of sin	Temple of Heaven, Beijing, reputedly set on live tortoises, which could survive for 3,000 years and preserve wood	Tortoises are exploited by mariners for food

1835	1878	1918	1930S
Darwin observes differences among tortoises on the Galapagos Islands	In Belgium, tortoise fossils found with iguanadons at depths of 322 metres	Death of a Marion's tortoise imported into Mauritius from Aldabra in 1766 – the oldest reliable record for longevity	Conservation concerns expressed. Tortoises feature in advertisements.

LATE 6TH CENTURY BC	625–600 BC	c. 500 BC	c. 450 BC

Aesop's fable *The Hare and the Tortoise*

Silver staters of Aegina, the first European trade coinage, have a turtle/tortoise in relief

Zeno's paradox of Achilles and the tortoise:

$$\frac{10d}{t} = \frac{100+d}{t}$$

Tortoise = symbol of longevity in Confucius' *Analects*

1643	17TH CENTURY	18TH CENTURY	1789

Humpty Dumpty = a tortoise?

Tortoise sculptures in Italian piazzas. To Calvinist Christians a symbol of modesty in marriage

Vogue in France and elsewhere for Boule furniture inlaid with tortoise shell

Gilbert White's *Natural History and Antiquities of Selborne* includes his inherited tortoise, Timothy

1950S	1959	1983	1984	2002

Cartoon character Bert the Turtle advises US citizens to 'Duck and Cover' in the event of a Soviet atomic attack

Charles Darwin Foundation for the Galapagos Islands

The Colour of Magic, the first volume in Terry Pratchett's Discworld series, is based on the ancient myth of the world resting on a turtle

European Economic Community ban on importation of three species of Mediterranean tortoises

World Chelonian Trust incorporated.

World Turtle Day – which includes tortoises – on 23 May is the birthday of Linnaeus

References

1 FITTEST NOT FASTEST

1 Evan T. Sage, trans., *Livy* [History of Rome] (London, 1935), bk 36,
 chap. 2, p. 251.
2 Michael J. Connor, 'The Pancake Tortoise', *Tortuga Gazette*, 28/11
 (1992), pp. 1–3.
3 Hesketh Pearson, *The Smith of Smiths* (London, 1948), p. 302.
4 Charles Darwin, *Journal of Researches into the Geology and Natural
 History of the Various Countries Visited by HMS 'Beagle'* (London,
 1839), entry for 26–7 September 1835.
5 Justin Gerlach, *Famous Tortoises* (Cambridge, 1998), p. 29.
6 Bob Langton, *British Chelonia Group Newsletter*, 125
 (September–October 1998), pp. 3–4.
7 H. Rackham, trans., *Pliny: Natural History* (London, 1940), book
 IX, p. 12.
8 Darwin, *Journal of . . . HMS 'Beagle'*, entry for 26–7 September
 1835.
9 Bernard De Voto, ed., *Letters from the Earth* (New York, 1938),
 Letter VIII, p. 38.
10 Darwin, *Journal of . . . HMS 'Beagle'*, entry for 26–7 September
 1835.
11 *Ibid.*
12 Gerald Durrell, *The New Noah* (London, 1955), pp. 80–82.
13 *The Scotsman* (21 July 2000).

14 *The Times* (20 May 1966).

15 *The Times* (30 January 1930).

16 Letter in *The Times* (30 January 1930).

17 Gerlach, *Famous Tortoises*, p. 7; *Daily Telegraph* (23 November 1998).

18 *The Times* (8 December 1999).

19 Gerlach, *Famous Tortoises*, p. 42.

20 Sylvia Townsend Warner, *The Portrait of a Tortoise, Extracted from the Journals of Gilbert White* (London 1981), p. 36.

21 *Ibid.*, p. 46.

22 Deborah Cadbury, *The Dinosaur Hunters: A Story of Scientific Rivalry and the Discovery of the Prehistoric World* (London, 2000), pp. 80–89.

23 *Ibid.*, pp. 171–5. Mantell's essay was published in the *Edinburgh New Philosophical Journal* and *The American Journal of Science*.

24 Darwin, *Journal of . . . HMS 'Beagle'*, entry for 26–27 September 1835.

2 MYTHS AND SYMBOLS

1 Edward Gibbon, *Decline and Fall of the Roman Empire*, chap. xxv, Reigns of Jovian and Valentinian, note.

2 Peter Bently, *The Hutchinson Dictionary of World Myth* (London, 1996), p. 86.

3 J. C. Cooper, ed., *Brewer's Myth and Legend* (London, 1992), p. 287.

4 J. C. Cooper, *An Illustrated Encyclopaedia of Myths and Symbols* (London, 1993), p. 175.

5 Cooper, *Brewer's Myth*, p. 287.

6 Margaret Stutley and James Stutley, *A Dictionary of Hinduism* (London, 1977), p. 157.

7 Kenneth McLeish, *Myths and Legends of the World* (London, 1996), p. 240.

8 Bently, *The Hutchinson Dictionary*, p. 113.

9 Jean Chevalier and Alain Gheerbrant, *The Penguin Dictionary of Symbols* (London, 1996), p. 1017.

10 Cooper, *Brewer's Myth*, p. 287.

11 Stutley and Stutley, *Dictionary of Hinduism*, p. 157.

12 Chevalier and Gheerbrant, *Dictionary of Symbols*, p. 1017.

13 Bently, *The Hutchinson Dictionary*, p. 34.

14 Chevalier and Gheerbrant, *Dictionary of Symbols*, p. 1017.

15 *Ibid.*, p. 1016.

16 *Ibid.*, p. 1018.

17 Frederic Raphael, *Literary Review* (June 200),p. 13.

18 Chevalier and Gheerbrant, *Dictionary of Symbols*, p. 1017.

19 Quoted in Sir James Frazer, *The Golden Bough* (1890, revd 1911–15), vol. I, p. 169.

20 Cooper, *Brewer's Myth*, p. 287.

21 *Ibid.*, p. 287.

22 Chevalier and Gheerbrant, *Dictionary of Symbols*, p. 1019.

23 Quoted in Frazer, *The Golden Bough*, VOL. I, p. 170.

24 Cooper, *Illustrated Encyclopaedia*, p. 175.

25 Chevalier and Gheerbrant, *Dictionary of Symbols*, p. 1019.

26 Jan Knappert, *Pacific Mythology* (London, 1995). p. 304.

27 His Divine Grace A. C. Bhaktivedanta Swami Prabhupāda, trans., *Bhagavad-Gita As It Is* (1986), 5. 26, pp. 302–3.

28 Knappert, *Pacific Mythology*, pp. 303–4.

29 Powys Mathers, *The Book of the Thousand Nights and One Night* (London, 1964), pp. 202–9.

30 Cooper, *Brewer's Myth*, p. 287.

31 Nadia Julien, *The Mammoth Dictionary of Symbols* (London, 1996), p. 459.

32 Robert Graves, *The Greek Myths* (London, 1960), vol. I, pp. 63–5.

33 Shelley, *Hymn to Mercury*, ix.

34 John Ruskin, *Lectures on Art* (London, 1905), vol. xx, p. 389.

35 Chevalier and Gheerbrant, *Dictionary of Symbols*, p. 1019.

36 *Ibid.*, p. 1018.

37 Elphinstone Dayrell, *Folk Stories from Southern Nigeria, West Africa* (London, 1910), no. 22, pp. 79–80.

38 Frazer, *The Golden Bough*, vol. IX, p. 31.

39 *Ibid.*, vol. I, p. 151.

40 *Ibid.*, vol. I, p. 155.

41 *Ibid.*, vol. XIII, p. 140.

42 www.zelva.cz

43 Titus Burckhardt, *Siena: The City of the Virgin* (Oxford, 1960), pp. 117–21.

44 Gibbon, *Decline and Fall*, chap. lxviii, 'Reign of Mahomet the Second', note 13.

45 C. P. Farrell, ed., *The Works of Robert G. Ingersoll* (New York, 1902), vol. xi, p. 338.

46 Michael Frayn, *The Russian Interpreter* (London, 1966), p. 19.

47 Salmon Rushdie, *Midnight's Children*, book 2: *My Tenth Birthday* (London, 1981), p. 195.

48 Robert Southey, *A Common-Place Book*, series II (1849), p. 570.

49 http://www.heldlikesound.com/tortoise6.html

50 Tony Crisp, *The New Dream Dictionary* (London, 1994).

51 David Pickering, *Dictionary of Superstitions* (London, 1995), p. 263.

52 *The Times* (4 October 1963).

53 http://www.ananova.com/news/story (7 December 2000).

3 ANCIENT AND MODERN

1 Charles Singer, E. J. Holmyard and A. R .Hall, *A History of Technology* (Oxford, 1954), vol. I, pp. 29–30, 132–4.

2 Joseph Needham, *Science and Civilisation in China* (Cambridge, 1956), vol. II, pp. 347–50.

3 Simon Leys, trans., *The Analects of Confucius* (New York, 1997), 5. 18.
4 S. A. Handford, trans., *Fables of Aesop* (London, 1954), no. 64, p. 68.
5 *Ibid.*, no. 65, p. 69.
6 T. W. Rhys Davids, trans., *Buddhist Birth-Stories; or, Jataka Tales* (London, 1925), pp. viii–x.
7 *Folk Tales from China*, second series (Peking, 1958), pp. 9–12.
8 Jonathan Swift, *Gulliver's Travels*, ed. Paul Turner (Oxford, 1998), part ii, chap. 8.
9 Handford, *Fables of Aesop*, no. 66, p. 70.
10 Marianne Moore, trans., *The Fables of La Fontaine* (New York, 1954), pp. 126–7.
11 *Ibid.*, pp. 238–9.
12 William Makepeace Thackeray, *Pendennis* (1848), chap. 21.
13 Anita Brookner, *Hotel du Lac* (London, 1993), p. 27.
14 Constance Garnett, trans., *War and Peace* (London, 1971), p. 887 .
15 Lancelot Hogben, *Mathematics for the Million* (London, 1951), pp. 308–9.
16 Rackham, trans., *Pliny: Natural History*, book ix, p. 13.
17 Caesar, *The Conquest of Gaul*, trans. S. A. Handford (London, 1951), p. 76.
18 Gibbon, *Decline and Fall*, chap. xlvi, 'Troubles in Persia'.
19 *Oxford Magazine* (16 February 1956).

4 EXPLOITATION

1 Joan S. Schneider, *The Desert Tortoise and Early Peoples of the Western Deserts* (Riverside, 1996).
2 Ivor Noël-Hume and Audrey Noël-Hume, *Tortoises, Terrapins and Turtles* (London, 1954), p. 14.
3 Daniel Defoe, *Robinson Crusoe* (London, 1994), p. 110.

4 Donald M. Frame, trans., *The Complete Works of Montaigne* (London, 1958), p. 584.

5 Noël-Hume and Noël-Hume, *Tortoises, Terrapins and Turtles*, p. 15.

6 *Ibid.*

7 *Ibid.*

8 Hesketh Pearson, *The Smith of Smiths* (London, 1948), p. 96.

9 *Encyclopaedia of World Art* (London, 1972), vol. IX, pp. 704–5.

10 *Ibid.*, vol. III, p. 737.

11 Carole Seymour-Jones, *Painted Shadow: The Life of Vivienne Eliot* (London, 2002), p. 44. The verses were first published in 1996 in *Inventions of the March Hare*, edited by Christopher Ricks.

12 *The Times* (18 April 1938).

13 Letter in *The Times* (8 December 1938).

14 Letter in *The Times* (9 December 1938).

15 Letter in *The Times* (16 December 1938).

16 J. K. Rowling, *Harry Potter and the Prisoner of Azkaban* (London, 1999), p. 48.

5 APPRECIATION

1 John Scott, ed. and trans., *Love and Protest: Chinese Poems* (London, 1972), p. 62.

2 Joseph Needham, *Science and Civilisation in China* (Cambridge, 1956), vol. II, p. 524.

3 *Ibid.*, vol. V (1980), pt 4, p. 291.

4 *Ibid.*, vol. V (1983), pt 5, p. 158.

5 Fitzroy Maclean, *Back of Beyond* (London, 1974), p. 118.

6 *The Connoisseur Complete Encyclopaedia of Antiques* (London, 1975), p. 429.

7 *Miller's Antiques Encyclopaedia* (London, 1998), p. 163.

8 Quoted by Aylwin Guilmant, *Sussex of 100 Years Ago* (Stroud, 1991), p. 117.

9 *Oriel College Record* (1991), p. 28.

10 Gerald Durrell, *My Family and Other Animals* (London, 1956),
pp. 52–5.

11 *The Times* (20 August 1960).

12 *The Times* (10 September 1987).

13 Balzac, *Les Paysans* (Paris, 1855), chap. x; as *Sons of the Soil*, trans.
Katharine Prescott Wormeley (Champaign, 1998).

14 David Magarshack, trans., *Crime and Punishment* (London, 1951),
p. 45.

15 In Edgar Faure, *The Serpent and the Tortoise* (London, 1958), p. xvi.

16 Stella Gibbons, *Cold Comfort Farm* (London, 1932, repr. 1938), p. 12.

6 CONSERVATION

1 *The Times* (19 January 1962).

2 *The Times* (26 February 1964).

3 *The Times* (2 August 1972).

4 *The Times* (3 December 1982).

5 *The Times* (6 July 1972).

6 *The Times* (16 November 1978).

7 *Daily Telegraph* (20 April 1979).

8 *Daily Telegraph* (24 July 1979).

9 *Daily Telegraph* (2 November 1979).

10 Sherif and Mindy Baha El Din, *Status of the Egyptian Tortoise in
Egypt*, Tortoise Trust Web 1994.

11 *Daily Telegraph* (20 August 1999).

12 *New York Times* (11 September 1999).

13 *British Chelonia Group Newsletter*, 119 (September–October 1997).

Bibliography

Cecchini, Giovanni, *The Palio and the Contrade* (Siena, 1958)

Cotterell, Arthur, *A Dictionary of World Mythology* (London, 1979)

Dean, Judy, *Dictionary of World Myth* (London, 1995)

Desmond, Adrian, and James Moore, *Darwin* (London, 1991)

Gordon, Stuart, *The Encyclopaedia of Myths and Legends* (London, 1993)

Grzimek's Animal Life Encyclopaedia, vol. VI: *Reptiles* (New York, 1975)

Ions, Veronica, *Indian Mythology* (London, 1983)

Larson, Edward, *Evolution's Workshop* (London, 2001)

Magnan, Philippe, and Jerome Maran, *L'Encyclopédie Terrariophile, Tortues*, vol. I (Mommenheim, 1999)

Norman, David, *Prehistoric Life* (London, 1994)

Oxford Dictionary of Natural History (Oxford, 1985)

Shaughnessy, E. L., ed., *New Sources of Early Chinese History* (Berkeley, 1997)

Associations

Since the mid-twentieth century, more tortoise conservation and welfare organizations have been formed – locally, nationally and internationally. Most are staffed by dedicated volunteers and depend on modest subscriptions, donations and sale of tortoise-related items. Some of the better known groups are the following:

American Tortoise Rescue, 23852 PCH, Suite 928, Malibu, California 90265, USA

British Association of Tortoise Keepers, Edgbaston Hotel, 323 Hagley Road, Birmingham, B17 8ND, England, UK

British Chelonia Group, P.O. Box 1176, Chippenham, Wiltshire SN15 1XB, England, UK

British Tortoise Trust, B.M. Tortoise, London WC1 3X4, England, UK

California Turtle and Tortoise Club, CCTC Westchester Chapter, Box 90252, Los Angeles, California 90009, USA

Chicago Turtle Club, 6121 N. Fairfield Avenue, Chicago, Illinois 60659, USA

Gulf Coast Turtle and Tortoise Society, 1227 Whitestone, Houston, Texas 77073, USA

National Turtle and Tortoise Society Inc, P.O. Box 66935, Phoenix, Arizona 85082, USA

New York Turtle and Tortoise Society, NYTTS RO, P.O. Box 878, Orange, New Jersey 07051–0878, USA

Ontario Turtle and Tortoise Society, P.O. Box 52149, 307 Robinson Street, Oakville, Ontario, Canada, L6J 7N5

Reno Tur-Toise Club, P.O. Box 8783, Reno, Nevada 89507, USA

Traffic International, 219c Huntingdon Road, Cambridge, CB3 ODL, England, UK

World Wide Fund for Nature UK, Panda House, Weyside Park, Godalming, Surrey, GU7 1XR, England, UK

Websites

A Cupulatta: info@acupulatta.com
American Tortoise Rescue: www.tortoise.com
British Chelonia Group: www.britishcheloniagroup.org.uk
California Turtle and Tortoise Club: www.tortoise.org
Chicago Turtle Club: www.geocities.com/~chicagoturtle
Desert Tortoise Preserve Committee: www.tortoise-tracks.org
Dutch Turtle and Tortoise Society: www.igr.nl/users/nsv
Gulf Coast Turtle and Tortoise Society: info@gctts.org
Irish Association of Tortoise Keepers:
    http://homepage.tinet.ie/~090316
Mid Atlantic Turtle & Tortoise Society: www.matts-turtles.org
New York Turtle and Tortoise Society: www.nytts.org
Slowcoach: www.slowcoachap.org.uk
SOPTOM: www.tortues.com
TortoiseAid: www.tortoiseaid.org
The Tortoise Keepers Association: www.tortoisekeeper.co.uk
Tortoise Trust: www.tortoisetrust.org
Traffic International: www.traffic.org
World Chelonian Trust: www.chelonia.org

Acknowledgements

This pioneering project of uncovering a cultural history of tortoises would have been impossible without help. My own tortoise, Timmy, provided inspiration. Friends and acquaintances offered many useful pieces of information, illustrations and suggestions for exploring other sources in such a diverse subject. Apologies if I have omitted any thanks from the following list.

I am grateful to the following individuals: Barbara Abbs, Kath Baldwin, Jean Bates, Tom Berthon, Jan Creaye, Brian Dennis, Rosalind Fiamm, Jack Fitzpatrick, Mary Flynn, Tom Flynn, Ian and Maria Fowler, Professor Philip Grierson, Adam and Monica Guy, Pat Hopper, Anna Johnston, Philip Knights, Lawrence Long, Pippa Lord, Peter Lovesey, Bill McMillan, Nina Malm, Helena Martinova, Douglas Matthews, Virginia Monson, Chris Mullen, Margery and Peter Nash, Krisztina Nyitrai, Phillipa Pearce, Terry Quinn, Ian and Jenny Revell, Pina Scalera, Ted Schoeters, Richard Scrope-Howe, Jean Smith, Peter Stein, Karen Townend, Margaret Townend, Pat Tucker, Wang Tao, Bill and Cherry Tibbles, Deryck Weatherall, Holly Willis, Judy and Simon Young, Stephanie Zarachap.

I have received help from these institutions: the German and Thai embassies in London; The British Library; Cambridge, Crawley and Croydon public libraries; the libraries of the Italian

Cultural Institute, the universities of Cambridge, Harvard (especially Betty Furdon of Property Information Resource Center) and Sussex, of Gonville and Caius College, Cambridge, the London Library, and the School of Oriental and African Studies, (University of London); from the British Museum, Booth Museum of Natural History, Institut royal des Sciences naturelles de Belgique, Natural History Museum, Wakefield Museums and Arts; and The Cultural Archive, Brighton; Guillain-Barré Support Group of the United Kingdom; Oriel College, Oxford (archivist Elizabeth Boardman); Royal Society for the Prevention of Cruelty to Animals; Tortoise Trust; Traffic International; and the United States Information Service.

Photo Acknowledgements

The author and publishers wish to express their thanks to the below sources of illustrative material and/or permission to reproduce it:

Photos courtesy of Roger Balsom: pp. 36, 37, 48; photos courtesy of Jean Bates: pp. 9, 93, 105 (left), 126, 177; © 2002 John Bell, All Rights Reserved (<http://members.aol.com/johnbell77>): p. 22; courtesy of Bosch Marketing Communications: p. 171 (right); photos by permission of the British Library, London: p. 43 (Or. 4769 f.10); photos © British Museum, London: 55, 76, 77, 84, 85; courtesy of Carlton Cards: p. 171 (left); photo courtesy of Barry Carpenter: p. 111; courtesy of Citroën UK Ltd: p. 172 (foot); photo courtesy of the Contrada della Tartuca, Siena: p. 65; The Culture Archive: pp. 57, 117, 139; photos courtesy of A. Cupulatta: pp. 12, 20, 21, 24; photo Diageo Archive/© Guinness UDV 1936 (The GUINNESS word and HARP device are trade marks): p. 172 (top); photo courtesy of Edinburgh Zoo: p. 170 (top); photo courtesy of Ian Fowler: p. 66; photo courtesy of Maria Fowler: p. 173; courtesy of the Guillain-Barré Syndrome Support Group: p. 178; photos courtesy of Adam Guy: pp. 67, 68; photo courtesy of Clive Harman: p. 162; photo courtesy of Alan Hoole: p. 16; photos courtesy of the Horniman Museum, London: pp. 93, 105 (left); by permission of the Houghton Library, Harvard

University: p. 60; courtesy of Tony Husband: p. 170 (foot); photos courtesy of Mike Jessop/Ash Veterinary Surgery, Merthyr Tydfil: pp. 154 (foot), 156, 157 (top); photo courtesy of Kingsway Electrical Company: p. 169; photos: Koninklijke Bibliotheek, The Hague (Ms KA 16, folios 112v b1 (p. 63, top) and 110v a1 (p. 63, bottom)); photo courtesy of McCormick Tractors International Ltd: p. 81; photo courtesy of Virginia Monson: p. 113; photo courtesy of the Museum in Docklands, London (PLA Collection): p. 100; illustration courtesy of Peter Nash (after J. F. Horrabin) p. 86 (top); photo by David Paterson, courtesy of Ian Hamilton Finlay: p. 121 (top); photo courtesy of Michael Portway/Taylor & Portway Ltd: p. 121 (foot); photo © Robert Quest: p. 158; photos courtesy of Rob Reynolds/Seers Croft Veterinary Surgery, Faygate, Sussex: pp. 149, 154 (top), 155; photos © RMN – C. Jean: pp. 118, 119; Royal Cabinet of Paintings 'Mauritshuis', The Hague: p. 6; photo courtesy of Roger Scammell/Gore Cross Veterinary Clinic, Bridport: p. 157 (foot); photos courtesy of Siva Singham: pp. 49, 50, 116; design by Tortoise (layout assistance by Sheila Sachs): p. 71; photos courtesy of the Tortoise Trust: pp. 105 (right), 108; courtesy of TurtleWax® Inc.: p. 174; photo: Wakefield MDC Museums and Arts (Wakefield Museum, Yorkshire): p. 109; photo courtesy of Lesley Walton: p. 175; photo courtesy of Deryck Weatherall: p. 33; photo: Bunty Young: p. 114; photo courtesy of Simon Young: p. 168; photos taken by an undercover photographer, 2002: pp. 101, 102.

Index